LIGHTHOUSES OF GREATER LOS ANGELES

LIGHTHOUSES
OF GREATER
LOS ANGELES

Rose Castro-Bran

THE History PRESS

Published by The History Press
Charleston, SC
www.historypress.net

First published 2015

Manufactured in the United States

ISBN 978.1.60949.619.7

Library of Congress control number: 2015958836

Notice: The information in this book is true and complete to the best of our knowledge. It is offered without guarantee on the part of the author or The History Press. The author and The History Press disclaim all liability in connection with the use of this book.

CONTENTS

ACKNOWLEDGEMENTS

This book was only made possible with the generosity and assistance of the following individuals and groups. I would like to thank Tom Budar of the Point Fermin Lighthouse Society and the Cabrillo Beach Boosters; Dennis Drag, PhD, of the Long Beach Lions Club; Paul Mandeville of the Long Beach Lions Club; Charles Johnson of the Ventura County Museum of History and Art; Dr. David Rosen, U.S. Coast Guard historian; Jeff and Richard Gales of the U.S. Lighthouse Society; Joanna Bard Newton; Anne Hansford and Joe McKenzie of the San Pedro Bay Historical Society; the late Dorothy Ramirez and Helen Brant of the Hueneme Historical Society; Long Beach Library Historical Archives; Merrill McCauley of the National Park Service; Joel Anderson of the Anderson Design Group, Inc.; and John M. Ambicki Jr.

In grateful appreciation to the members of the United States Coast Guard Aids to Navigation Team Los Angeles/Long Beach.

Special thanks to the children and descendants of lighthouse keepers for sharing their stories and their lives: Linda Cherney, Jerry Boylan, Heather Reed, Margaret Kellogg-Anderson, Martha McKenzie and to the late Laverne White-Dornberger (for ten years of being my pen pal).

Special acknowledgement and thanks to Eric Castro-Bran, my father in-law, fellow auxiliarist and "keeper" of the Point Vicente Lighthouse for over twenty years, for his encouragement, support and resources.

Thank you to my husband, Kim, for your endless help and support and for being my light.

INTRODUCTION

The Greater Los Angeles Area encompasses five counties in Southern California, including Los Angeles, Orange County, San Bernardino, Riverside and Ventura. Dotting the coastlines is a handful of lighthouses ranging from intrinsically ornate to starkly modern. Similar to the diversity that Los Angeles is known for, each lighthouse represents a different period in history, an altering demand for change and modernization, as well as the progression of technology and optics. The history of lighthouse progress throughout Los Angeles, in some cases, applauds preservation and restoration and, in other cases, surrenders to the advancements of its time. Each lighthouse is a time capsule of the era in which it was constructed, and each fulfilled or continues to fulfill its primary purpose of guiding vessels through safe passage.

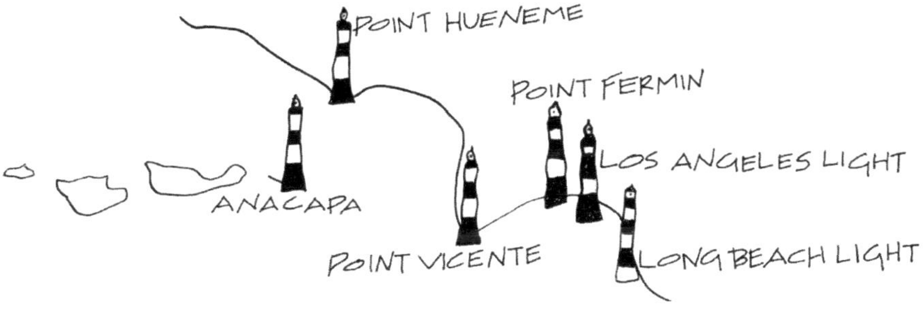

Author's sketch.

INTRODUCTION

Lighthouses of Greater Los Angeles illustrates the story of six federal aids to navigation, beginning with two lighthouses that were both illuminated on the same day, Point Fermin and Point Hueneme Lighthouses, followed by Los Angeles Harbor Lighthouse (Angel's Gate), Point Vicente Lighthouse, Anacapa Island Light Station and Long Beach Light, as well as the U.S. Coast Guard. A community effort, Lions Lighthouse for Sight in Long Beach, a private aid to navigation, is depicted as well.

Chapter 1

POINT FERMIN LIGHTHOUSE

EARLY YEARS

The Tongva/Gabrielino were the first people to inhabit the Los Angeles Basin. According to a Tongva/Gabrielino elder, "We each had our communities, but we were all neighbors and there were no boundaries. We would go to each other's places to gather and to trade." Though they had an ancient respect and understanding that we are of the land, land claims and acquisitions would soon supersede this noble understanding. As the "first people," they were given the name Gabrielino by the Spanish, and it has remained. The Gabrielino were avid hunters and gatherers and thrived in a coastal region that was rich in natural resources and endless sunshine. They inhabited vast areas of the Los Angeles Basin for several thousand years dating back to around 6000 BC.

It was fifty years after Christopher Columbus, in the year 1542, that Juan Rodriguez Cabrillo set out for exploration and landed in America. Sailing north from Mexico into unknown waters, Cabrillo was on a journey to acquire land for the King of Spain.

On October 8, 1542, the hillsides of what was to be Rancho San Pedro were under heavy dark plumes of smoke. Chaparral, which consisted of tangled shrubs and bushes, created a dense and attractive habitat for the California grizzly bear, so clearing the area by burning the chaparral was a periodic necessity, and as a result, dark plumes could be seen for miles out to sea. Juan Rodriguez Cabrillo witnessed the billowing smoke and, from this,

A statue of Juan Cabrillo on display at Cabrillo Beach, San Pedro, California. *Courtesy San Pedro Bay Historical Society.*

named the bay *Bahía de los Fumos* or "Bay of Smokes," a title that was held for over fifty years.

Upon arriving on the shores of San Pedro, Cabrillo was greeted by the Tongvas. Cabrillo's ambitions were extensive as he was seeking to discover a route to Asia and the Spice Islands; search the area from the Pacific Ocean to the Atlantic, known as the mythical Strait of Anian; chart the coast; and, like most explorers, discover gold. Of these ambitions, Cabrillo was successful in claiming over eight hundred miles of coastline for Spain. Cabrillo is given credit, based in part on his voyage, for a west-to-east Pacific crossing some twenty years later. Once the world's continents were connecting, the Spanish age of exploration would give way yet again, this time to the colonial era.

Sebastian Viscaino sailed into the bay on November 26, 1602—a day he believed was in celebration of Saint Andrew—and changed the name to *Ensenada de San Andrés* or "Bay of Saint Andrew." It was, however, in 1734, that Cabrera Bueno, a famed navigator and cosmologist, discovered that the day Viscaino arrived was actually on the feast day of Saint Peter, not Saint Andrew. Once again, the bay was renamed—this time for the martyred Saint Peter, translated as San Pedro.

Since Saint Peter was also bishop of Alexandria, Egypt, the same location that the first lighthouse was reported to be established by the pharaohs in 280 BC, the name was serendipitous, as in due time, San Pedro would also have its own lighthouse, and the bay of San Pedro would be illuminated again—this time not from burning bushes but from a lighted beacon.

The prominent point, which sits at the tip of the Palos Verdes Peninsula, was given the name Point Fermin by Captain George Vancouver in recognition of Father Fermín de Francisco Lasuén de Arasqueta, who served as father and president of the California missions.

This was only the start for San Pedro, and by the mid-1830s, it had become the most important port on the Pacific coast. One challenge that remained for the shallow bay was that ships would risk running aground and, as a result, would have to drop anchor about a mile off shore. Transferring cargo and passengers into smaller boats posed several capsizing disasters. Fortunately, from a makeshift dock and landing at the base of the cliffs, ships would be able to load and discharge their goods. This would later be known as Sepulveda Landing, in recognition of the Sepulvedas, who had the foresight to construct the dock. One of two geographical points of the area during this time was Deadman's

Island. This area would later be dredged and absorbed into the current breakwater. The second area was Rattlesnake Island, which today is Terminal Island.

The Mexican War, also referred to as the Mexican-American War, came to an end in 1848. The passageway up and down the newly acquired California coast was described repeatedly by mariners of the time as isolated, dangerous and unpredictable.

In 1851, Phineas Banning, originally from Delaware, left Philadelphia, where he was working in his brother's law firm, and arrived in San Pedro, California. Banning and George Alexander became partners and began making profits operating a stagecoach service from San Pedro. When Banning discovered that the Sepulveda Landing was bought out by August Timms, and the name was changed to Timms' Landing, Banning grew suspicious.

Timms's land purchase, along with Banning's newfound awareness that Washington would soon declare San Pedro an official port of entry with its own customhouse, spurred him into action. Banning bought up a tract of land from the Sepulveda's, directly near Timms' Landing, and had his own wharf constructed, appropriately called Banning's Landing. In November

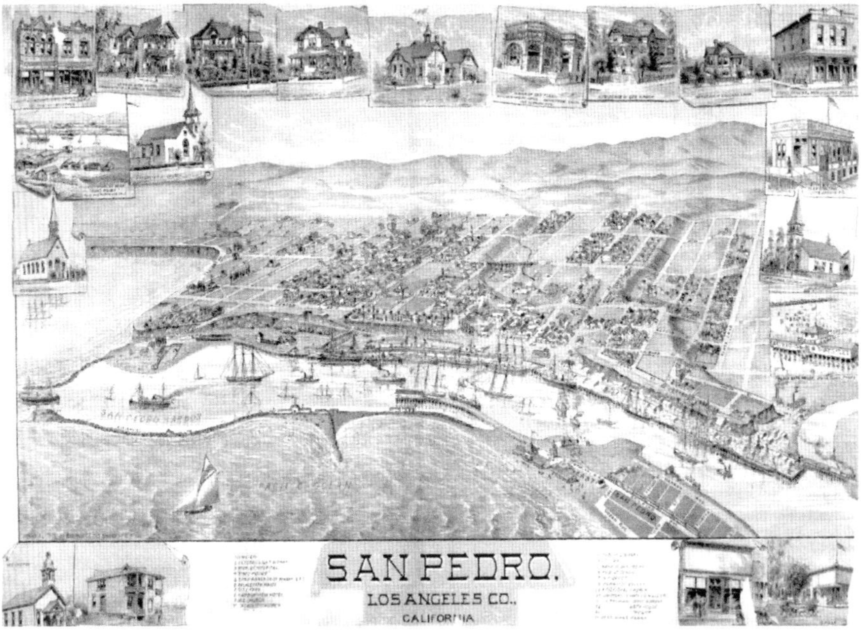

Artist's conception of San Pedro Harbor, 1893. *Author's collection.*

1854, Banning, along with a group of investors, purchased 2,400 acres adjacent to San Pedro for port expansion. Banning would name the city after his Delaware birthplace, Wilmington.

The gold coast of California would see more than sunshine when gold was discovered in 1849. The rush for this raw mineral brought with it an influx of vessel traffic, first to San Francisco Bay and then expanding farther down the coast. That same year, Congress employed the U.S. Coast Survey to identify the most important points up and down the Pacific coast that would necessitate illumination.

In 1861, Captain Phil Sheridan arrived and erected a military post at San Pedro. The reservation encompassed much of the Rancho Palos Verdes. Today it is known as Fort MacArthur and served as a U.S. Army post keeping watch over the Los Angeles area from 1914 to 1982.

Petitioning for a Light

As the Coast Survey cutter *Lawrence* explored the Pacific shoreline, it made its way down to San Pedro Bay in 1850. In 1852, Congress authorized for the construction of sixteen lighthouses along the Pacific coast. Point Fermin, however, was not one of them.

Phineas Banning recognized that an aid to navigation to the new port would undoubtedly guide mariners his way and successfully petitioned the U.S. Lighthouse Service to build a lighthouse. However, as a result of ongoing land disputes and funding, his request would be held up for fifteen years before construction could even begin. By 1872, the site had been officially selected. Ships were utilized to bring in loads of redwood and fir, which were then delivered to the site.

An excerpt from the *Wilmington Enterprise* on November 5, 1874, reads: "Thomas Winship, of San Francisco, lampist of this coast, has arrived and is now engaged in putting up the lamp on the lighthouse at Point Fermin, which will be completed by the close of the week. This is the finishing task upon one of the best constructed houses in the county, and perhaps, as good a lighthouse as can be found on the coast."

Finally, on December 15, 1874, Point Fermin was illuminated. The total cost was approximately $20,000 for the lighthouse and fog signal.

In sync with Point Fermin illuminating the California coast on this day, its "twin" or "sister" lighthouse, Point Hueneme, also turned its light on

The Point Fermin Lighthouse in San Pedro, California. *Courtesy San Pedro Bay Historical Society.*

for mariners this day. The two lighthouses were constructed from the same plans with only slight variations.

The wood used for framing of the lighthouse consisted of Douglas fir, and California redwood was used for the siding and trim. The new style was innovative in that it would incorporate the best resources of the area.

The architect responsible for this unique design, which afforded accommodations for both the lighthouse keeper and assistant keeper along with their families, was Paul J. Pelz. Pelz served as chief draftsman of the Lighthouse Board and is perhaps best known as the designer of the Library of Congress in Washington, D.C.

The Victorian-era design is referred to as Swiss Carpenter Gothic or, most notably, Stick Style. The ornate structure is known for its decorative cross beams, gabled roofs, ornate trusses, projecting bays and hand-carved porch railings. It is a wood-frame, residential-style lighthouse. The lighthouse is about 50 feet tall, sits on a 100-foot cliff and is approximately 150 feet above sea level.

In total, there were six "sister" lighthouses that were constructed using Pelz's design. Five of these lighthouses remained close, as in proximity. They were constructed on the West Coast, with only one, Hereford Inlet Lighthouse, constructed on the East Coast. Of the six lighthouses, three

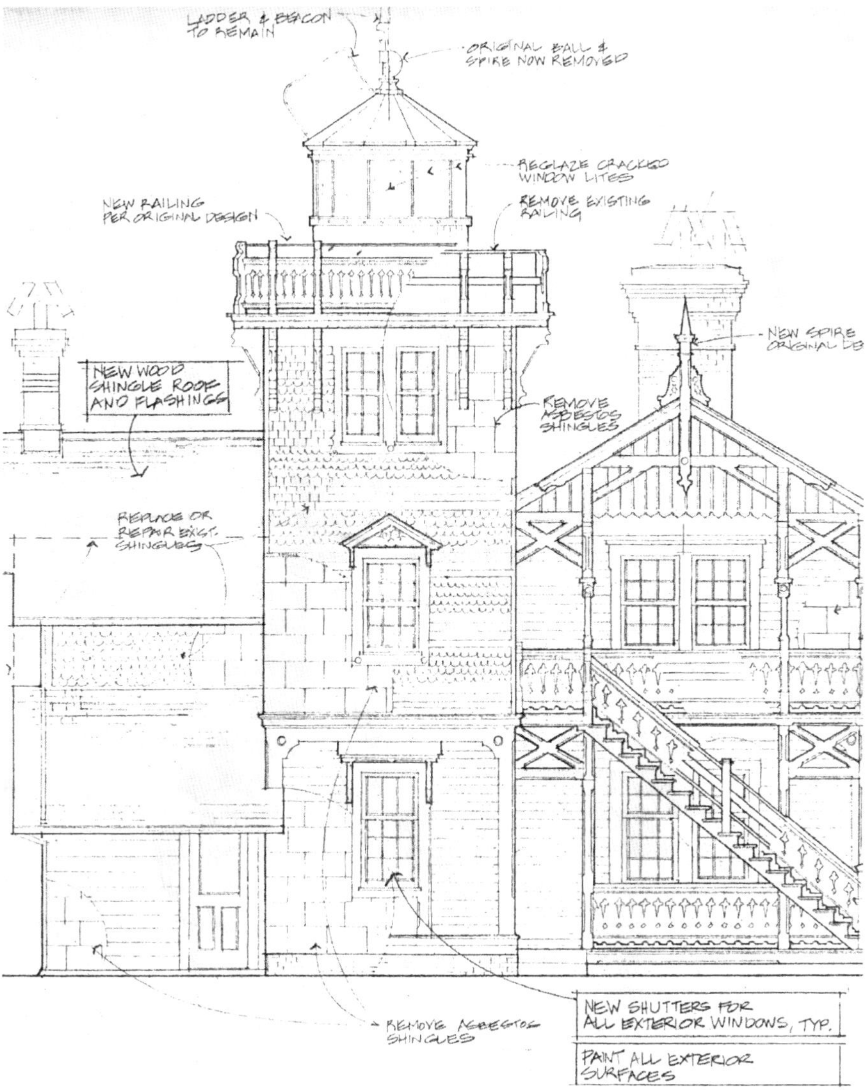

Blueprint of the Stick-style lighthouse. Point Fermin would be one of six lighthouses built from these plans. *Courtesy Eric Castro-Bran.*

are still standing. In addition to Point Fermin Lighthouse, East Brother Island Light in Richmond, California, currently serves as a bed-and-breakfast with periodic day access available. Hereford Inlet Lighthouse narrowly survived a severe storm in 1913 and is currently open to the public.

Welcome Harbor City Festivities, April 1908. *Courtesy San Pedro Bay Historical Society.*

Typically, the keeper and his family lived on the first floor, and the assistant keeper and his family lived on the second floor. A unique design with separate entrances in both the front and rear of the lighthouse afforded both families easy and private accessibility to their quarters.

Progress continued throughout the area during this time with the advancement of the railroad. The year 1869 brought with it the completion of a railway connecting Los Angeles and Wilmington (inner San Pedro Bay). That same year, the transcontinental railroad was completed. In 1888, San Pedro was officially incorporated and became a city.

The British ship *Respigadera,* which reportedly came too close to the cliffs of Point Fermin, crashed into the jagged rocks in 1888 and went aground. The fog signal, which had been planned, was never established at the site. On April 1, 1889, the light was changed from flashing red and white to fixed white.

The tower would have two lens changes prior to the final fourth-order Fresnel lens that was installed in 1912. The light would shine about twelve to fifteen miles into the distance.

Minding the Light

The lighthouse, which sits on roughly three and a half acres, includes large overhangs and a porch area, ideal for sunny afternoons and gatherings. The first keeper and assistant keeper to enjoy the sights were not only women but also sisters. Mary L. and Ella T. Smith took over lighthouse keeping duties in October 1874. When the sisters arrived at the lighthouse, there was not a welcoming beacon to greet them, as the Fresnel lens was not to be installed until the following month. This did, however, give the sisters a few weeks to acclimate to the lighthouse before minding the light. Wilmington was the closest town for the sisters, followed by the pueblo in downtown Los Angeles.

Though most reports reveal that the sisters left the lighthouse in 1882 due to loneliness and isolation, an article titled "Patronage, Politics and Preference," by Henrietta E. Mosley and Kristen Heather, points to the possibility that the women were pressured out of their position "by an ambitious would-be successor" and undoubtedly would have been replaced by a male counterpart.

F. Ross Holland, one of this country's foremost authorities on lights, has noted that keepers during the 1800s "at one time or another had female assistant keepers; and a surprising number of women as principle keepers." Female lighthouse keepers were traditionally paid less than their male counterparts, making them more desirable from a cost-saving perspective. Wives working alongside their husbands would sometimes take over their duties following their passing or would serve as assistant keepers.

The sisters were diligent in their duties and brought with them prior lighthouse experience, as they had served together at the Ediz Hook lighthouse in Washington Territory, and per keeper logs, were diligent in their duties. Whatever their reason for leaving, they will always be recognized as the first keepers of Point Fermin and were both extremely qualified and efficient.

The next notable keeper was Captain George N. Shaw, who was originally from Cambridge, Massachusetts. In *The First Light Keeping Families at Point Fermin*, Henrietta Mosley states, "When the Civil War began in 1861, he joined the 20th Massachusetts Volunteer Infantry, a regiment containing many distinguished Bostonians that suffered heavy casualties at the Battle of Balls Bluff, an early defeat for the Union." Captain Shaw was wounded during his service and consequently had loss of mobility in two of his fingers. As a result of this injury, he was transferred to gunboat service on the Mississippi River. Following further health issues, Captain Shaw was granted a medical discharge and returned home in 1863. After a speedy recovery, he was able to serve again in the army, continuing his service until the end of the war.

Further excerpts related: "Shaw joined the Lighthouse Service in San Francisco in 1877. He was first assigned to the Point Reyes Light Station and then served as assistant keeper at Yerba Buena Island Light Station. While stationed at Yerba Buena he married a young San Francisco woman, Carrie Merrell."

Captain Shaw served at Point Fermin Lighthouse from 1882 to 1904. His service as a Civil War veteran and his experience as a sea captain proved to be beneficial, as he would have to mind the light, keep long hours of watch for ships in distress and take care of the house and grounds. Shaw and his family enjoyed many a party at the lighthouse, inviting guests from all over the area. His presence continues to live on in the lighthouse as the Point Fermin Historic Society periodically re-creates, through living history during events, his service at the lighthouse. In addition to 1882 being the year that Captain Shaw took over as keeper, it also shows growing progress as the year that San Pedro was founded. Captain Shaw and his family would also witness further growth when San Pedro received its incorporation as a city just seven years later.

Whale oil was the primary fuel used by all lighthouses in the 1800s. The Lighthouse Service was turning to cost-efficient alternative sources of fuel, such as kerosene. This helped in availability and supply. In 1898, the Point Fermin lamp would receive a technological improvement called the incandescent oil vapor (IOV) lamp. This replaced the dated lamp mechanism, helping to produce an improved and brighter light. These new lamps, in conjunction with new steam-powered ships of the time, were notable improvements.

The elaborate lighthouse design would not be complete without a lush garden surrounding it. Currently, the well-manicured garden consists of a variety of various flowers and shrubs. Many of the plants over the years have included roses, daisies, lilies, ferns, hydrangeas, lavender, blue salvias, flax and Japanese maple, to name of few—a fitting Victorian-period garden.

It is a sharp contrast to what the grounds would have been like when the lighthouse was first constructed. The area plants were mainly desert plants such as cacti, sage scrub and ice plant. Rainwater was crucial and was carried from the rain gutters into three brick cisterns constructed on the site. The cisterns were able to hold a combined twenty-four thousand gallons of water, with the largest of the three at ten thousand gallons and the smaller two at seven thousand gallons. The keepers would then pump the water using a hand pump.

As President William McKinley symbolically pressed a button in the White House in 1899, thousands of people converged on the lighthouse grounds to watch as the railroad cars simultaneously dumped rocks to build the breakwater.

Fortunately, in 1907, a water tower and windmill were installed, making life a little easier for J.H. (Irby) Engles, who served as keeper from 1904 to 1917. In 1912, the light was changed to flashing white in order to distinguish it from other lighthouses.

There was a windmill in operation behind the lighthouse, with a ladder affixed for easy access. The windmill was removed later when it was no longer needed.

Engles would have witnessed the entire transition from hand pump to water tower to finally, in 1906, piped water to the site, thanks in part to the San Pedro Water Company. Population growth and increased housing development in the area spurred the demand for piped water.

Protection and Expansion

The nearby Fort MacArthur was established in 1914. It became the headquarters post for the harbor defense installations designed to protect the Los Angeles Harbor area. Located on the "Upper Reservation" of Point Fermin were the heavy-duty seacoast gun emplacements.

The Point Fermin Park was established in 1925 through the generous donation of George Peck to the City of Los Angeles for use as a park. The property was originally a part of the Sepulveda family land holdings. The park is composed of thirty-seven acres and today is surrounded by mature trees; solid concrete arbors, ideal as shelter from the sun or for picnics; a promenade; a small amphitheater; and a children's playground. The park's tiered pathways would lead visitors down to the cliff bottoms and a bathhouse. The cliff paths were subsequently closed due to eroding cliffs, costs and safety issues. The number of reported deaths from the cliff over the years is highly disturbing, with many visitors ignoring posted warning signs in an effort to see below.

The keeper at the time was William "Willie" Austin (1917–25), who served along with his wife, Martha, and their eight children. The eighth child was named Paul "Fermin" Austin in honor of his birthplace at the lighthouse. In total, they had ten children, seven of whom would reach adulthood.

The Austin family had served at Point Arena Lighthouse in Mendocino County, followed by Point Conception Lighthouse in Santa Barbara County. The lens duties would have been a bit of a relief for the Austins when they arrived at Point Fermin compared to Point Conception since a first-order Fresnel lens (like that at Point Conception) is about eight and a half feet tall compared to a fourth-order lens, which is just under two and a half feet tall. Prior to electricity, the entire lens routinely needed to be cleaned of soot.

The mid-1920s would bring even more progress. The Austins had the privilege of witnessing electricity come to the light and a flashing electric bulb, which equaled greater efficiency but also signaled that their position would soon start to become obsolete.

Daughter Becomes Keeper

This sketch depicts the youthful, vibrant keeper Thelma Austin in the lantern room of Point Fermin Lighthouse. *Courtesy Kim Castro-Bran.*

In 1925, Martha Austin passed away, with William passing only two months later, reportedly from a "broken heart." It was Thelma Austin, their daughter, who petitioned the U.S. Lighthouse Service to take on the duties of head lighthouse keeper—a position that her twenty-one years of experience at the lighthouses left her readily qualified to fulfill. In a heartfelt plea, she wrote, "Why, the sea and this lighthouse seem to me like a holy shrine, and I'm afraid it would break my heart to give it up. But no matter what happens, I will accept my fate with a brave heart, and just as cheerfully as my parents would have done. When you have been raised in the

Young ladies in costume at a lighthouse celebration. *Courtesy San Pedro Bay Historical Society.*

lighthouse atmosphere, as I have been, it is mighty difficult to change your mode of living and accept any other line of endeavor which does not offer romance and adventure." Thelma was granted the position and, along with her sister Juanita, carried on the lighthouse tradition, bringing both youth and vigor to the light.

Lighthouse keepers and assistant keepers between 1874 and 1927 were all federal employees and were each paid a modest salary along with a small stipend of food supplies. In addition to the salary, the keepers and their families were allowed to live in the lighthouse quarters. Many keepers and their families maintained gardens and livestock to get by.

Legacy Continues

One might think that when the sisters left the light two years later, their legacy would have come to an end. However, their bloodline continues. Martha Austin McKinzie, granddaughter to Martha and William Austin, continues to keep their legacy and sacrifice alive. Martha, a San Pedro native, has served as president of the Point Fermin Lighthouse Society for over a decade. Martha has been instrumental in piecing together the history and helping to preserve this historic landmark. She has been able to retrace the steps of both her grandparents and aunts as they diligently gave their service and has documented their trials and tribulations from the keeper's log, photographs and stories that have been handed down, some directly from her father, who was raised at the lighthouse.

Lighthouse Illumination

As light is emitted from its light source, it travels in different directions at varying rates of speed and is composed of different color invisible to the human eye. Augustin Fresnel positioned each prism to capture the light rays as they traveled, and as the light would pass through the glass, the light would refract or bend and would then be redirected and magnified through the glass in a straight beam. The result was extraordinary, with the ability to project light out to sea for miles and miles. The center rays, as they did not need to bend, would travel through the glass and, therefore, would only need to be magnified. Untold amounts of lives have been saved from his invention. In addition, studio lighting and car headlights blossomed from Fresnel's design.

As Point Fermin Lighthouse was the first lighthouse to illuminate the San Pedro Bay on December 15, 1874, the history of the lens is equally impressive. The lens was made in France from hand-carved glass prisms and is named for its inventor French physicist Augustin Fresnel. From France, the lens was first shipped to New York prior to arriving in California.

Augustin Fresnel, designer of the Fresnel lens. *Courtesy U.S. Lighthouse Society.*

The characteristics of the Point Fermin's first Fresnel lens displayed a red-and-white flashing beacon until the year 1888. It was then decided by the U.S. Lighthouse Board to change the light to a fixed fourth-order beacon. Unlike the rotating beacon that would create a flashing light, the fixed light would give off a steady beam. With the growing harbor expansion and an uptick in vessel traffic, the light would once again return to a rotating Fresnel lens in 1912.

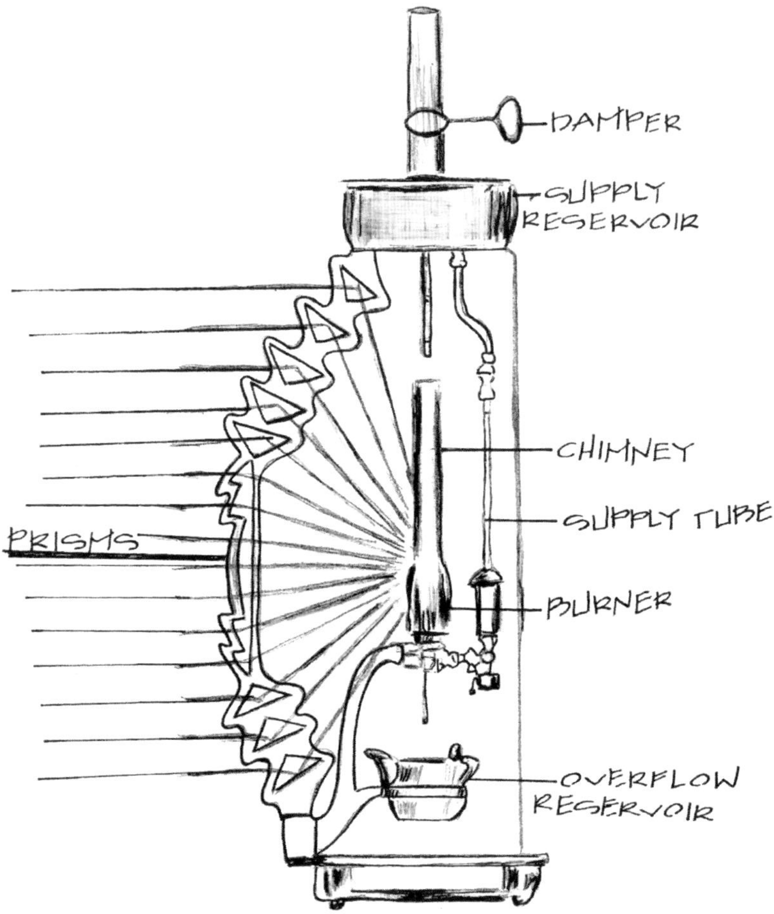

This sketch of the mechanics of the Fresnel lens show the various components that the keeper needed to continually check, refill and repair on occasion. *Author's sketch.*

The Fresnel lens rotated on a pendulum or "clockworks" system from the base of the rotating lens attached to ropes, pulleys and weights that would descend straight down the tower all the way to the first floor. This required the keepers to routinely climb the stairs to the top of the tower, fill the oil reservoir, trim the wick and crank the weights and pulleys back to their original position so that the light could start rotating again. This procedure would need to be done periodically throughout the night. In 1927, following an agreement with the federal government, the City of Los Angeles assumed operation of the lighthouse. A groundskeeper for the city was assigned to the lighthouse and would turn the light on each evening.

John Olguin

One notable citizen of San Pedro was John Olguin. John started in the lifeguard service in 1937 and worked his way up to Cabrillo Beach lifeguard captain and finally became the director of the Cabrillo Beach Museum in 1949, serving until he retired in 1987, becoming the director emeritus of the Cabrillo Marine Museum. John lived in San Pedro for over eighty-five years and was instrumental in the lighthouse restoration. He is credited with thwarting off a possible demolition of the lighthouse in the 1970s.

It was John Olguin and Bill Olsen who together formed a preservation committee dedicated to the lighthouse preservation in the 1960s. Originally called the Point Fermin Lighthouse Committee, in 1974, the name was officially changed to the Point Fermin Lighthouse Society and has been in operation ever since. The group's lighthouse preservation and restoration efforts have been numerous through outreach, education and good old-fashioned hard work and elbow grease, this grass-roots effort has undoubtedly saved history.

With the construction of two nearby lighthouses positioned to illuminate the area, it was rumored that Point Fermin could become obsolete. But

John Olguin, seen here teaching local students about the marine ecology at the Cabrillo Aquarium in San Pedro. *Courtesy San Pedro Bay Historical Society.*

despite the whispers, the lighthouse would continue to illuminate into the distance. It was not, initially, the other lights that would extinguish Fermin's light but the darkness of war.

The U.S. Lighthouse Service existed as a federal agency from 1789 until 1939, at which time the Coast Guard absorbed the Lighthouse Service. Following that time, the U.S. Coast Guard would assume all aid-to-navigation duties. During World War II, all lighthouse personnel were given the option to enlist as military members of the Coast Guard or continue working as civilian employees.

War Years

With the bombing of Pearl Harbor on December 7, 1941, the U.S. Navy gave orders for a coastal blackout. The concern was that the light would serve as a beacon for enemy vessels. The light was extinguished two days

The aerial photo with the sentry point affixed reveals why the Point Fermin lighthouse was ideal. *Courtesy U.S. Coast Guard.*

later and was subsequently removed from the tower in 1942. Following this sudden and mandated blackout, the Fresnel lens would never return to the tower, nor would it ever be lit again.

The navy took over the grounds during World War II and converted the station into a signal tower and a radio station. The pristine white lighthouse was repainted to a camouflaged-green color in 1942. Albeit less attractive, the new color caused the lighthouse to fade away in the background of shrubs and trees, creating a less visible appearance during war.

Point Fermin Lighthouse was reconfigured as a "lookout" during World War II. *Courtesy U.S. Coast Guard.*

Following the blackout, the lantern room and gallery were removed. They were replaced by a lookout shack "sentry point," or observation post, the primary objective of which was to keep watch for any enemy vessels. This unsightly but necessary addition during that time would remain affixed to the lighthouse for the next thirty years. The new construction was also dubbed by locals as the "the chicken coop" due to its unsightly, barn-like appearance.

With the observation deck, the navy had sweeping views of the ocean from both directions. It was positioned high above the cliff, was somewhat segregated from residences and was afforded some additional cover from trees and shrubs.

The building in front of the lighthouse was built by the navy during World War II. It was used for radio and sonar equipment and temporary military housing, as well as lifeguard housing.

Point Fermin was no longer the main light for the harbor. Los Angeles Harbor Lighthouse had become the main illumination for the harbor entrance.

Missing Lens

Following these events, the lens was believed to have been relocated to the basement. It was only after the war was over that interest was regained in restoring the lighthouse. It was at that point that the roughly 250-pound lens was discovered to be missing.

In relation to the missing lens, John Olguin is quoted as saying, "No one in San Pedro knew, but it's not easy to lose a lens that big." The mystery of the missing lens would turn to a "cold case" for many years. What did remain was a hole in the lantern room that served as a constant reminder of where the Fresnel lens and drive mechanism were once housed.

Coast Guardsman LCDR Edison Fabian had suggested from witness accounts that the lens was seen in a nautical museum on the Santa Monica Pier. However, the nautical museum was closed after violent winter storms destroyed a large portion of the pier in 1983.

Fortunately, the owner of the nautical museum was a well-known Santa Monica lifeguard captain named Captain George Watkins. Watkins was given or loaned the Fresnel lens and displayed it in his Santa Monica Pier Museum. After the museum closed, Watkins then moved the light to his home in Malibu. Watkins's home was known for its famous parties, and the likes of movie stars such as Marilyn Monroe were seen at his Malibu beach hideaway parties.

Watkins continued his passion for collecting nautical artifacts and displayed many of them in his private residence. The Fresnel lens had a prominent location at his home—that is, until after his death. Again, the lens went missing, only to reappear this time in the window of a real estate company in Malibu, California. The owner, Louis Busch, had known Captain Watkins for many years. They were personal friends.

After Captain Watkins passed away, his son delivered the lens to Busch, stating, "This is what my father wanted you to have." Delighted by his new treasure, Busch proudly displayed the lens in the window of his Malibu real estate office for many years and, to his credit, took impeccable care of the lens.

Once the lens resurfaced, Busch was quickly contacted, but he was not convinced that this was, in fact, the missing lens. It was a gift from his good friend, plus there were also more fourth-order Fresnel lenses in this country than any other size lens. Not to mention, Busch had grown quite fond of the lens.

It would take years of patience and fortitude from the folks of the Point Fermin Lighthouse Society, who spearheaded the efforts, along with support from the Coast Guard, U.S. Coast Guard Auxiliarist and Attorney Joanna Leighton Nevesny, Jim Woodward, Huell Howser and many more people behind the scenes.

Lighthouse curator Kristen Heather was able to procure a detailed 1912 photo of Point Fermin's Fresnel lens and lantern from the National Archives in Washington, D.C. Attorney Leighton Nevesny compared the 1912 photo to a photo of the lens in Busch's window.

Busch, however, was still not exactly convinced it was a match, so a Washington, D.C. law firm was brought in to digitally enhance and enlarge the photographs and match up all the screws from the two photographs. From this, the firm was able to prove that the lenses were one in the same.

In addition, Jim Woodward, a Coast Guard veteran and Fresnel lens expert, gave the final confirmation and expert analysis, saying, "Each lens is totally unique to where the placements of the screws are. They are hand drilled and tapped. This is a fingerprint of the lens. No two Fresnel lenses are the same because of the fasteners. It is a perfect match." It was at this point that Busch was convinced that the lens did belong to Point Fermin Lighthouse and was happy to return the light to its rightful home. In late November 2006, Jim Woodward meticulously secured the final details in place for the lens to come full circle and return to Point Fermin.

This story of lighthouse history had a happy ending. The Fresnel lens is proudly displayed on the first floor of the lighthouse museum. Once

The fourth-order Fresnel lens was housed in the lantern room. It is now displayed on the first floor of the lighthouse. *Courtesy Kim Castro-Bran.*

the original lens is gone, there really is no feasible way of replacing it. They are hand-made sculptures and scientific marvels that have withstood the test of time and have saved countless lives. Each lens is positioned at a specific angle to capture and project light. The advantage of where the lens is located is that visitors can walk around the entire lens, which is protected by a see-though cover, and are able to witness this historic treasure.

Efforts to Preserve and Protect

In 1972, Point Fermin was added to the National Register of Historic Places, and in 1974, with the commemoration of the lighthouse's 100th birthday, a new wooden lantern room was reconstructed. This new lantern room was due to the collaboration of Bill Olsen and John Olguin, along with community support.

In 1999, the City of Los Angeles spent $2.7 million to transform the lighthouse into a public museum, and in 2002, the City of Los Angeles, the Port of Los Angeles and the State of California all contributed funds in order to have the lighthouse restored and retrofitted for public access on November 1, 2003. In 2002, an exact duplicate of the original lantern room was successfully completed. The impressive new lantern room gives visitors a complete area view, with the added benefit of seeing Los Angeles Harbor Lighthouse in the distance. On clear days, visitors can also see both Santa Barbara and Santa Catalina Island.

On May 2, 2012, Point Fermin Lighthouse was added to the National Historic Lighthouse Preservation Act of 2000, which allowed "for eligible federal, state, and local agencies, non-profit corporations, educational agencies and community development organizations to be used for educational, recreational, cultural, or historic preservation."

Though the lighthouse was able to survive time, weather, war, earthquakes and even a missing lens, there was yet another unexpected hazard on the horizon—people. As the lighthouse is nestled away in a park, it has been, unfortunately, vulnerable to vandals. This time, however, it was the community that came to the rescue of the lighthouse. In particular, Julian Jimenez, a former park maintenance supervisor for the city of Los Angeles Department of Recreation and Parks, made it his mission to preserve and protect the lighthouse. In late 1979, Julian moved into the lighthouse. He

Above: A group of students from Los Angeles Unified School District are seen participating in group and outdoor activities during summer camp in 1972. *Courtesy San Pedro Bay Historical Society.*

Left: Seen here reenacting lighthouse life, Julian Jimenez and Martha Austin McKinzie continue education and preservation of this landmark. They and their spouses are active members of the Point Fermin Lighthouse Society. *Courtesy Kim Castro-Bran.*

was succeeded by a line of park maintenance supervisors who have lived at the lighthouse ever since.

In addition to his duties, Julian was very community oriented. Instead of a keeper keeping watch on the horizon, Julian was keeping watch on the lighthouse. For over twenty-two years, Julian minded the grounds and area parks. Regardless of whether the threat was vandals or bureaucracy, Julian, along with lots of community support and the Point Fermin Lighthouse Society, helped to preserve this rich and historic landmark. He is proof that one man can make a positive impact on saving history.

East of the lighthouse is a structure that was once the Point Fermin Café. Today, it is used by the American Cetacean Society (ACS), which helps to educate the public about whales. The American Cetacean Society is a nonprofit organization and, since 1967, has been dedicated to protecting whales (more specifically, the marine mammal of the order of cetacea: whales, dolphins and porpoises). The organization named an auditorium in honor of John M. Olguin. The society is regularly seeking volunteers. For more information, please visit www.acs-la.org.

Visiting the Light

As visitors arrive, there are a total of fifty-eight steps to the top of the tower. When entering the lighthouse, visitors today are received in the front parlor. This is typical for a federally run lighthouse. However, when Captain Shaw resided here, he reversed rooms and received guests through the backdoor and rear parlor—understandably, as the front parlor has the best view of the ocean.

From the front parlor, guests are then led into the back parlor. A custom cupboard in the back parlor shows the handy craftsmanship of the third keeper, Mr. Engels. He also constructed a built-in dish cupboard in the closet in the opposite corner. During the 2002 restoration, the closet was removed, and the original door was found preserved behind the cupboard. The main focal point in the back parlor is the recently recovered Fresnel lens.

Although the lighthouse was built to house two keepers and their families, two families never resided there simultaneously. The kitchen was used as a family gathering area, with a wood-burning stove, which was attached to the large chimney. There was plenty of work, including cooking, dishes, laundry and canning preserves.

A view of the stairs descending from the lantern room. *Courtesy Kim Castro-Bran.*

The second-floor master bedroom once served as a full kitchen but was removed by Mr. Engles in 1904. A second kitchen was not necessary, and once removed, the space allowed for an extra bedroom with a coal-burning stove for heat.

The second floor has a small room once used as a nursery and later a bedroom. A large room was built to be used as a living room but was traditionally used as the keeper's office. There is another bedroom, often referred to as the "Boys' Room," containing a rope bed of that period—hence the expression, "Good night. Sleep tight."

Visiting Today

In early 2012, the government deemed the lighthouse as "surplus property," or property that is no longer viable for government use and due to cost factors and other considerations can now be appropriated to other organizations that will work toward preservation and historical and/or educational purposes. An additional benefit is that donations or monies raised can go directly to these goals. After narrowing down the options to five viable groups, it was announced in early 2015 that the selected party would be the City of Los Angeles. The Point Fermin Lighthouse Society continues its work at the lighthouse.

The lighthouse is located inside the area of the Point Fermin Park, currently a historic park, at the end of Gaffey Street. There is a short walk from the parking area to the lighthouse.

Volunteer docents give visitors a tour starting from the outside grounds and lead guests up the front stairs, through the very detailed and ornate porch and in through the front door. Visitors are then guided into every room of the lighthouse, up the stars and into the light tower. The view alone is worth the visit. It is also recommended to visit the gift shop during your visit.

As the lighthouse is located inside Point Fermin Park, it is a great place for a picnic or to relax prior to or following the tour. The Point Fermin Lighthouse Historic Site and Museum is managed by the City of Los Angeles, Department of Parks and Recreations. The Point Fermin Lighthouse Society routinely does special events at the lighthouse such as luncheons, garden parties, beer and wine tastings, Easter egg hunts, Spooky Night on Halloween, night-time full-moon tours and much more, and on December 15 each year, the Point Fermin Lighthouse Society membership hosts a birthday party for the lighthouse. Membership in the Lighthouse Society is available and entitles the holder to a 10 percent discount on all purchases at the gift shops, plus other surprises. The above events routinely change, so please visit the below mentioned website for event updates and additions.

Driving Directions: 807 Paseo Del Mar, San Pedro, CA 90731
From the 110 Freeway south, take the Gaffey Street exit at the end of the freeway, bearing left onto Gaffey. The lighthouse is located four miles ahead in the Point Fermin Park at the end of Gaffey Street.

For the Point Fermin Lighthouse Society website, please visit www.pfls.org.
For the City of Los Angeles's website, please visit www.pointferminlighthouse.org.

Chapter 2

POINT HUENEME LIGHTHOUSE

In October 1542, ships commanded by Juan Rodríguez Cabrillo sailed between Anacapa Island and the coastline today known as Ventura County. Those on these ships were the first Europeans to visit the area, though not its first inhabitants.

The area was already populated for hundreds of years by the Chumash people or, as they referred to themselves, "the first people." The Chumash are a Native American tribe who inhabited mainly southern coastal regions from Santa Barbara and Ventura to as far south as Malibu, as well as many of the Channel Islands. Evidence of Chumash life in the area was reported by the children of the keepers living on the point, as they would find artifacts in the lighthouse area.

The name Hueneme or Wyneme (pronounced "Wy-NEE-mee") has origins dating back to the Chumash people. It means "resting place" or "midway point."

Father of the Port

As Thomas Bard arrived in 1865, the town of Hueneme was already sowing the seeds of a strong farming community. With a keen vision in mind, in 1872, Bard formally laid out the town. In an effort to preserve the original Chumash name, Bard listed the original spelling of the name, Hueneme, as the town's official name.

Thomas Bard drilled for and discovered oil in Ojai, enabling him to turn his attention to his dream of building a wharf at Hueneme. Upon hearing news of a submarine canyon called Hueneme Canyon offshore of Ventura, Bard knew immediately commerce would come. The canyon is about one thousand feet deep and just over one mile wide at certain points. The natural water flow would automatically carry out any resting silt, making the canyon an ideal location for a wharf. Bard moved forward, undeterred by strong opposition, and spent years planning and negotiating.

Thomas Bard, visionary and "father of Port Hueneme." *Courtesy Joanna Bard Newton.*

Finally, in 1872, he succeeded in giving the city its own wharf called Hueneme wharf (also referred to as Bard's wharf which allowed for the berthing of large vessels). This made way for Hueneme to become one of the largest and main shipping ports on the Pacific Coast for years to come. The many vessels necessitated a lighthouse, which was erected in 1874.

In May 1891, the *Free Press Newspaper* reported, "The wharves and warehouses filled with the products of the country are a wonder to the casual visitor. It is all a scene of active life and enterprising industry."

Sugar Turns Town Sour

As Hueneme was on the fast track, Hueneme's citizens definitely smelled the sweet smell of success, but what seemed sweet would soon sour. In 1897, Henry T. Oxnard opened a sugar factory in the neighboring town

A postcard of the American Beet Sugar Factory in Oxnard, California. *Author's collection.*

and needed a large workforce. The solution was to pull employees from its neighbors—in particular, Hueneme.

With the quick and sudden growth of this new sugar enterprise, mass distribution was needed, and it came via the Southern Pacific Railroad. As more tracks were being laid, and with the completion of the Santa Susana Tunnel, San Francisco and Los Angeles were now quickly linked, and the vessel traffic to Hueneme Wharf slowed to a crushing halt.

Over the next two decades, Hueneme had morphed into what looked like a ghost town, and the supposed beach plans for Hueneme did not grow to expectations. Further frustrations mounted in 1906, when legal difficulties prevented the railroad from coming.

In 1911, the completion of the Panama Canal brought with it a renewed sense of optimism, and as a result, the wharf was extended in anticipation. However, the temporary gains in trade did not last. The final straw was the stock market crash of 1929, followed by the Great Depression.

ORIGINAL POINT HUENEME LIGHTHOUSE

The southern entrance of the Santa Barbara channel was the site selected for a lighthouse at Hueneme. It was, however, not the first choice. The low ground was viewed as not an ideal living location, as it was surrounded by lagoons and drifting sand. After much consideration, Hueneme initially won out over Anacapa, and on March 3, 1873, Congress allotted $22,000 for the construction of a lighthouse at Point Hueneme.

Construction began on April 25, 1874, by the firm of Salisbury and Company, and with the only difference the placement of a door and chimney, the Point Hueneme and Point Fermin lighthouse are almost identical. The structure included ten rooms and four fireplaces, and unlike at Point Fermin,

Original Fresnel lens that remained in operation until 1899. *Courtesy Ventura County Museum of History and Art.*

Point Hueneme Lighthouse grounds with a lighthouse service flag in the center of the photo. *Courtesy Point Hueneme Lighthouse Collection.*

where only the keeper and keeper's family resided in the lighthouse, at Point Hueneme, both the keeper, the assistant keeper and their families resided in the lighthouse.

The 1882 Annual Report of the Lighthouse Board stated: "It is important that a steam fog signal should be established here. The numerous passenger and other steamers, in going up and down the coast, pass inside Anacapa Island, and very near the coast, which here makes a considerable elbow. The land at this point is quite low, and is so for ten miles inland, so that it is difficult to see if there is any fog."

Prior to the exhibition of the Point Hueneme light on December 15, 1874, the newly appointed keeper, Samuel Ensign, proudly accepted his position. He was promoted from first assistant keeper at Pigeon Point Lighthouse in San Mateo County, California, to Point Hueneme's principal keeper. He made the journey of just over three hundred miles with his family by horse and buggy and arrived on November 9 of that year. He began writing the first notes in his keeper log and would be diligent in noting the wind, weather and any important events of the day.

The very next day following Keeper Samuel Ensign's arrival, he saddled up again, this time making his way to San Buenaventura in order to stock up on months' worth of necessary supplies and rations. In addition, he met with a "lampist," a person who specialized in the assembly, care and exhibition of the Fresnel lens, and, per the notes in the logbook, the lampist "got the light in good order." In the 1870s, Hueneme was described as booming, with clipper ships arriving from all parts of the globe.

Initially, the Fresnel lens would display a "fixed" light, which emits a steady white light absent of any flash. It remained fixed for the first fourteen years in operation. In 1889, the light was changed to fixed red. The Fresnel lens remained the same, except for a red cylinder that was added to create the red glow.

The second Fresnel lens to arrive was a revolving fourth order, which produced a flashing signal. Similar to facets of a diamond, this lens had a total of six sides or panels and made two complete revolutions per minute. Each lens would throw out a powerful beam of light every five seconds.

For the first month, a continued stream of visitors made their way over, anxious to see the new lighthouse and meet the new keeper and his family. On December 13, Samuel Ensign was at the dock in the late afternoon to meet his assistant keeper, Mr. Giles. He arrived with this wife and two sons on the steamer *Constantine* from San Francisco. The steamer was also loaded with cargo freight, including housewares for the station. The assistant keeper and his family made their way up the stairs and settled into their quarters on the second floor of the lighthouse.

December 15, the day of the exhibition of the light, was met with fanfare and was also coordinated with its sister lighthouse, Point Fermin Lighthouse. The term "sister lighthouse" is used when the style runs in the family, hence the term "sister."

The keeper's log reported: "A brand new station with brand new people." The waters off Southern California were now seeing new lights as they started to dot the course, up and down the coast, for the stream of vessels beginning to arrive. Only ten days after the exhibition, on Christmas Day, the lighthouse would experience its first death as the sister-in-law of Samuel Ensign, Mrs. J. Egan, passed away.

Ghost stories have always accompanied lighthouses. But as this structure was made mostly of wood, the creakiness and eerie sounds of the structure over the years were a standard occurrence, as reported by the children who once lived there.

The first few months in operation would see a blanket of fog for periods lasting about twenty-four hours. Giles was reprimanded, on more than one occasion, for sleeping on the job during his watch from midnight to sunrise. Giles would stay at Point Hueneme for only just over seven months—not

Keeper Charles Allen with his wife, Anna, and daughters, May and Melba, as seen in 1902. *Courtesy Ventura County Museum of History and Art.*

because he was demoted, but because he was promoted to principal keeper of Pigeon Point light.

The assistant keeper would receive his training by serving at many different stations in hopes to graduate to principal keeper. Transfers from one station to another were very common, depending on the need. Samuel Ensign served as principal keeper at Point Hueneme until 1878.

The lighthouse would also see a shift in the oil used to keep the Fresnel lens during this time. Kerosene became the principal illuminate, as it was both readily available and cheaper than the whale oil previously used.

F. McFarland replaced Samuel Ensign and stayed on for four years, followed by E.H. Penny (one year) and J.H. Glassby (eleven years). As new ports started to spring up, giving vessels other options to dock, it was during this time that Hueneme experienced a noticeable decline in ship traffic. In 1894, Charles Allen was transferred from Humboldt Light Station, north of San Francisco, to the Hueneme light, where he would serve as principal keeper for twenty years.

In 1900, his wife, Anna, gave birth to their second daughter, Melba, at the lighthouse. Following an unsuccessful business venture, Charles Allen and his family returned to lighthouse service again, this time at Point Conception lighthouse, and would remain there until his death in 1930.

In 1914, Keeper H. Rosendale served at the lighthouse during World War I, helped donate to the Red Cross for the war efforts and served a total of thirteen years at the lighthouse.

On March 5, 1915, Thomas Bard passed away and was heralded as champion for Hueneme expansion, as well as for his endless contributions and his work as a California senator. Bard also made a historical and generous donation of three hundred acres of his personal land in order to see his vision of a harbor for Hueneme fulfilled.

Walter White began his service as principal keeper in 1927 and would stay on until his retirement on November 30, 1948. It was during his tenure that he would undoubtedly see the most progress of any other keeper.

HARBOR DEVELOPMENT

It seems through all the hardship, the city was always hopeful, and hope was on the horizon with new crops: citrus and lima beans. The new crops spurred new interest, and Sunkist stepped in and built two large packing

Dredging began on the new harbor on January 24, 1939, by the Standard Dredging Company. *Courtesy Point Hueneme Collection.*

plants in Hueneme, employing more workers than any other employer in the city.

However, for Hueneme to completely bounce back, it needed a big draw. The plan was to build a harbor in the salt flats, an area that seemed impossible. There was fierce opposition to the project, and President Roosevelt added to the debate when he stated that "the notion was unsound."

Even with presidential opposition, Richard Bard carried on the fighting spirit of his father, Thomas Bard. Proving the viability of the project, a feasibility study was conducted and bonds issued to fund the project in the amount of $1.75 million. Within minutes, all available shares were immediately sold to investors.

The groundbreaking ceremonies for the Oxnard Harbor District at Hueneme were scheduled for the following month on February 4, 1934 at 2:00 p.m. Richard Bard shoveled the first soil on the momentous occasion, which drew large crowds.

Richard Bard spoke on the perils and triumphs of the new harbor and noted the main consideration for the harbor's success as: "The deep submarine valley close to shore with a low, flat area capable of being cheaply dredged; Small amount of capital needed to complete harbor compared to other commercial harbors; Creation for cheaper freight cost; and the creation of industrial or maritime development bringing in new wealth and employment."

Richard Bard is seen turning the first shovel for the new harbor on February 4, 1939. Keeper Walter White is to the right with white keeper hat, with his wife, Francis, and daughter, Laverne, to his right. *Courtesy Point Hueneme Lighthouse Collection.*

Richard Bard further stated, "New enterprises of this kind are always met with a certain amount of resistance and opposition and today we are laboring under abnormal conditions caused by the war, which may slow down the tempo of this development." Following the new harbor development, the name was officially changed to Port Hueneme.

By 1940, the newspapers declared Port Hueneme "the answer to dreams of industrialists who would like to move to Southern California where utilities and climate make production easiest and cheapest in the nation."

A two-day dedication ceremony for the harbor was held over the weekend of July 6 and 7, 1940. Port Hueneme is known as the only deep-water port between Los Angeles and San Francisco. Ventura County Harbor authorities and civic leaders were on hand, along with townsfolk

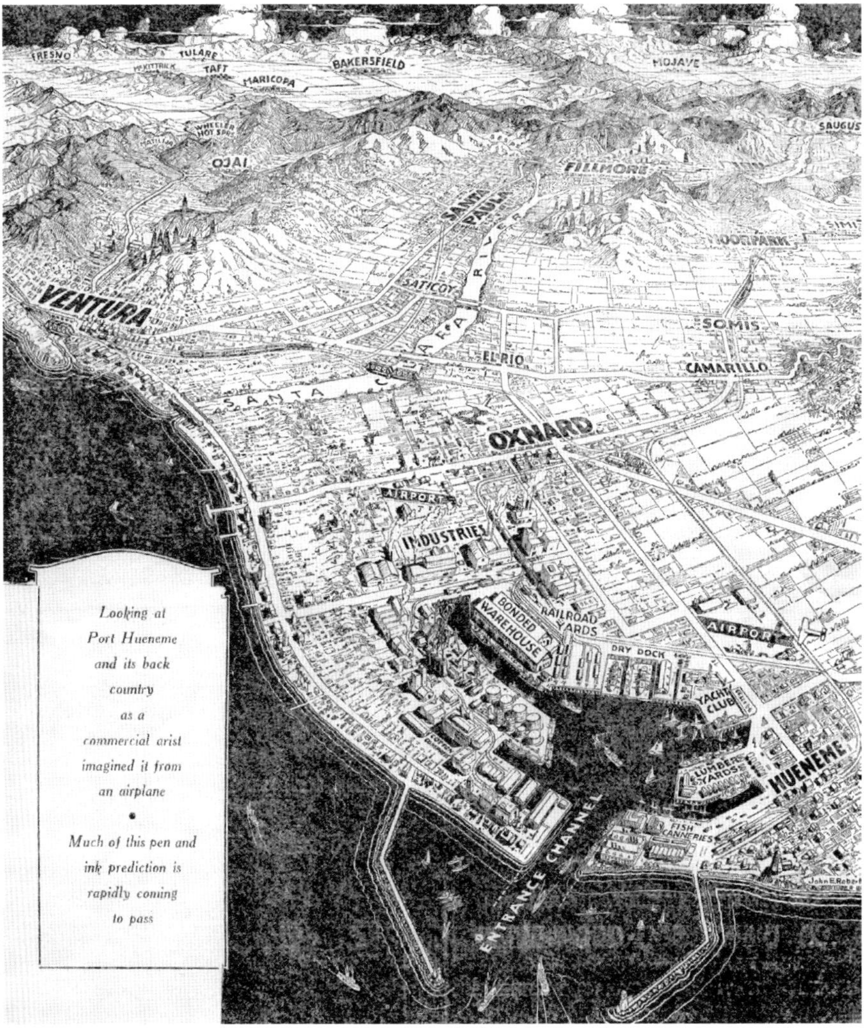

This 1929 artist depiction of what the future Port Hueneme Harbor would look like includes the area for the lumberyard, bonded warehouse and yacht club. *Courtesy Point Hueneme Lighthouse Collection.*

and area farmers, to welcome and watch as the first cargo vessel entered Hueneme's new harbor on January 4, 1941. The lumber freighter, the *Margaret Schafer*, unloaded 500,000 feet of lumber and also marked the end of a long labor strike.

Lighthouse Move

Nothing and no one could stand in the way of progress, not even a lighthouse. With the creation of the new harbors, the lighthouse light was no longer in a feasible location to illuminate the new entrance and would be in the way of development. Efforts were undertaken to move the original Hueneme lighthouse and make way for a new modern lighthouse planned for the east side of the harbor's entrance.

The solution was to move what was described repeatedly at the time as an "ancient structure" across the harbor. A bulldozer was brought in to remove huge piles of mud and sand from in front of the lighthouse, and a large rock barge was brought in to carry the lighthouse across the harbor. Workers had expressed concern that the job was too dangerous, and their concerns were realized when a wench line snapped back. Seven men narrowly escaped death, and the lighthouse slid back twelve feet.

The 104-ton lighthouse was moved on the barge in two phases between February 15 and 18, 1940. For the first move, workers waited for high tide, which was anticipated in the early morning hours. The sixty-six-year-old lighthouse was maneuvered to the middle of the channel and fastened to a derrick, where it rested for the second phase of the move. The second phase was scheduled in order to allow the press and spectators to witness the historic moment. John Brakey was the experienced house mover in charge of the undertaking and commented, "Time and tide wait for no lighthouse," alluding to high winds and conditions during the long process.

Captain Lebbeus Curtis, operating manager of Port Hueneme, commented, "Unlike Keeper Walter White, who regrets seeing the lighthouse go, I am exceedingly anxious for it to go." Sentiments were mixed. However, there were plans for the old structure. Clyde W. Jordan and P.H.L. "Doc" Wilson were the new owners of the lighthouse and planned to transform it into the new Hueneme Yacht Club.

In the ceremony, they were presented with the lighthouse flag by Francis White, wife of Keeper Walter White. Keeper White stood before the crowd and recanted the history of the lighthouse as he opened the original logbook from 1874 and read from previous keepers' words stories of maritime adventure, storms, gales, shipwrecks and commerce.

It was reported that the old lighthouse was to be kept intact, as its historical value would be evident in some fifty years. However, despite all its efforts, the Yacht Club would never came to fruition, and the structure was

Above: The lighthouse on a barge as it is ready to be moved across harbor. *Courtesy Point Hueneme Lighthouse Collection.*

Left: Walter White posed in his lighthouse keeper uniform. *Courtesy Point Hueneme Lighthouse Collection.*

eventually razed. It is believed that the toll the lighthouse structure suffered once removed from its foundation, coupled with the bombardment of wind and sand over the years, along with termite damage, as well as war, proved to be too much for the new yacht club.

Ironically, both the old and new Hueneme lighthouse share one very important design concept. Both designs represented one of the most innovative design concepts and technologies of its time, and conversely, they could not have been more opposite in design.

U.S. Navy Assumes Port Operations

The attack on Pearl Harbor changed the direction of the nation and port operations. In 1942, the U.S. Navy took control of the harbor and started a massive building program. Port Hueneme would soon become the second-busiest wartime harbor on the West Coast, and with it came a boom in the city's population.

By war's end, the port was at times busier returning men and supplies back home than it had been during the war. Port operations, however, still continued under the control of the navy. In March 1947, the city sought incorporation but lost by a narrow majority.

One year later, as the city was now able to use part of the harbor, incorporation succeeded. Despite its many challenges, the new city of Port Hueneme created its own police department, addressed the sewage and erosion issues, procured water flow from El Rio and made the area inviting to would-be residents. Richard Bard also spurred further growth by donating land for development.

In 1996, the port led the nation in citrus exports, and it is known for its continuous imports of foreign automobiles.

The New Light

A temporary light was erected prior to the completion of the new lighthouse on November 1, 1939, which was affixed to a steel structure. The new lighthouse was built in an Art Moderne style and was completed in December 1940. The structure that stands is forty-eight feet tall. Unlike

The Fairbanks-Morse engine and compressor combination, along with the fog signal timing device, which Keeper White is seen working on. Circa 1940s. *Courtesy Point Hueneme Lighthouse Collection.*

the usual concept of a lighthouse, it has a rectangular base and a square concrete tower that rises from a one-story fog signal building.

Two keepers' dwellings were built prior to the construction of the lighthouse, adjacent to the lighthouse, for the keepers and their families.

Walter White would be the only keeper to serve at both the original and current Point Hueneme Lighthouse for a total of twenty-one years of service. During the war, he was in charge of thirty-two men, and when the Lighthouse Service was absorbed by the Coast Guard, Walter White joined the Coast Guard as a civilian employee. On November 30, 1948, lighthouse keeper Walter White retired. His combined service took him to four light stations: Piedras Blancas, Point Montara, Point Arguello and Point Hueneme. In addition, he also served four years on a lightship, for a total of forty-five years of service.

Following Walter White's retirement, Leo Kellogg, who once served as assistant keeper at Anacapa Lighthouse was transferred as head keeper (civilian) at Point Hueneme

Portrait of Leo Kellogg in his keeper uniform. *Courtesy Port Hueneme Historical Society.*

While stationed at Anacapa Light, Joe May and Leo Kellogg became friends. As Joe was transferred to Point Vicente and Leo eventually was transferred to Point Hueneme, the two keepers would stay in contact and catch up on the events at each lighthouse.

A call was put out to a local doctor, Dr. Crites, in November 1952 because the keeper had taken ill and needed medical attention. Dr. Crites arrived at the lighthouse grounds and carried Keeper Kellogg to bed. Per the doctor's order, Kellogg remained in bed all day, but as night approached, Kellogg, determined to fulfill his lighthouse-keeping duties, got out of bed, against his wife's wishes, and turned the light on inside the lighthouse. Later that evening, at around 3:00 a.m., as he lay in his bed in the nearby keeper's quarters, he succumbed to a heart attack. Leo Kellogg served as the keeper at Point Hueneme from 1948 to 1952. Following Leo Kellogg's death, assistant keeper George Ward became the officer in charge and the final keeper at Point Hueneme Lighthouse.

SS *La Jenelle*

By the time the *La Jenelle* made its way to Port Hueneme, it had already gone through a number of name changes. Its final name, *La Jenelle*, was in honor of the new owner's wife. In a reported effort to avoid large dock fees, the owner had the 12,500-ton vessel anchored, attaching only one of its anchors to the ocean floor. On April 13, 1970, the anchor was no match against the gale-force winds and giant swells and began to drag. The two crewmen on board were helpless as the ship was carried away. Within minutes, the ship was wrecked off the beachfront west of the Port Hueneme breakwater. Crowds gathered daily to witness the stranded vessel, which would be pillaged and scrapped over the years.

Located just minutes from the lighthouse, a long narrow fishing jetty was built around the ship. Today, the rusted skeletal frame looks almost fossilized as large parts of it are now set into the jetty off Silver Strand Beach, and many times passersby don't even know what is on the other side of the jetty unless they take the time to look. More often than not, it is only the local fishermen and scuba divers who are aware of the wreck.

New State-of-the-Art Light

The Fresnel lens as seen in the lantern room prior to its relocation to the first floor. *Courtesy Kim Castro-Bran.*

Signs of wear and tear on the lens started to show in 2011. It would stutter for a few seconds and then start rotating again. As the signature flashes of the lens are reliant on a precise rotation, the flashing sequence was no longer reliable for mariners. The Coast Guard Aids to Navigation Team stepped in and kept servicing the light each time it would start to hesitate.

For over one hundred years, the Fresnel lens shone brightly, guiding boats along Hueneme's shores, but in August 2013, Point Hueneme's Fresnel lens took its last turn flashing in the tower and was relocated to the first floor in the lighthouse. One thing is certain: the faithful lens did its job and did it well.

A new state-of-the-art light is currently shining in the lantern room. After witnessing both the new lens in operation and the Fresnel lens on the first floor, visitors are able to see the showcasing of over one hundred years of technological advancements.

The new lens is a VLB-44 beacon and has tiers that can be added or subtracted depending on the intensity of light needed. The beacon is available from two to eight tiers and can be sized to the range of a particular application. Multiple tiers can be used to extend the range to sixteen nautical miles. Each tier uses about ten watts of energy, and colors include red, green, white, yellow and blue. The LEDs are precisely graded and placed to produce a light beam with minimum variation in intensity. A switch-mode regulator maintains the light output of the LEDs independent of input voltage and temperature.

Where flash characters are used, automatic Schmidt-Clausen correction occurs to increase the peak intensity to maintain the effective range of the beacon. Each beacon has up to fifteen programmable effective intensity options.

Port Hueneme Today

Today, Port Hueneme is a seaside community in Ventura County and is located sixty miles northwest of Los Angeles and forty miles south of Santa Barbara. It is also located in between what was once two large Chumash settlements, where today Malibu and Ventura are located.

Just outside the entrance to the Port of Hueneme is the Port Hueneme Historical Society Museum, originally the Bank of Hueneme. The museum is a Ventura County landmark, dedicated to showcasing the history of the area, which includes artifacts, photographs and displays. The building also houses the Port Hueneme Chamber of Commerce.

The Hueneme Beach Park is a spacious fifty-acre park and offers visitors walking paths between the flag plazas, gazebo and lighthouse, as well as other numerous recreational activities. It also hosts the Hueneme Beach Festival, which is held every August, with entertainment for the whole family.

The Hueneme Beach Sundial Memorial is in memory of Alaska Air Flight 261, whose passengers and crew members lost their lives near Anacapa

An aerial view of the Port Hueneme Harbor entrance with the lighthouse located in the foreground to the right of the channel entrance, circa 1950. *Courtesy U.S. Coast Guard.*

A postcard showing a navy vessel and recreational boats at the Port Hueneme Harbor. *Author's collection.*

Island on January 31, 2000. Names of each of the victims are inscribed on individual bronze plates secured on the perimeter of the dial.

The current Point Hueneme Lighthouse as seen from the beach. *Author's collection.*

Also close by is the U.S. Navy Seabee Museum, adjacent to Naval Base Ventura County (NBVC). Visitors can enjoy the rich history of the Naval Construction Force, better known as the SEABEES, and the U.S. Navy Civil Engineer Corps. Admission is free.

The entrance to the lighthouse is via the Lighthouse Promenade, which begins at the Flag Plaza on Surfside Drive (near the intersection of Surfside Drive and Ventura Road in the city of Port Hueneme). The Promenade walk is on a flat, paved road, and it is about half a mile to the lighthouse gate.

The U.S. Coast Guard Aids to Navigation Team Los Angeles–Long Beach (ANT LA–LB), along with the Coast Guard Auxiliary, offer monthly tours. For more information, please visit www.huenemelight.org.

Chapter 3

LOS ANGELES HARBOR LIGHTHOUSE (ANGEL'S GATE LIGHT)

The expansion of trade and the growth of goods moving in and out of the San Pedro Bay necessitated the building of a breakwater to form a harbor in 1899. Not long after, the need for a lighted entry for the new harbor brought about the decision by the U.S. Lighthouse Board to construct a lighthouse to mark the entrance to the burgeoning port in 1907. An interim light would guide the way, with the completion of the breakwater in 1910. It would be a few years before the funding was approved by Congress, and in 1912, construction on the lighthouse began.

The original plan was to have a wooden structure similar to those used at Southampton Shoals and Oakland Harbor. However, due to the forces of nature and the elements, this type of structure would not last long. The decision was made to construct the tower utilizing concrete, cement and metal. The approved structure was designed by Edward Woodruff, an assistant keeper in the U.S. Lighthouse Board. No other lighthouse was built with this design.

The lighthouse is constructed of steel plating, which is riveted to steel beams. The steel frame was manufactured by a local company, Llewellyn Iron Works in Los Angeles. The structure was placed on top of the pier head at the end of the San Pedro breakwater. The base of the lighthouse is an octagonal shape with metal plates and helps to offset the pounding waves.

The cylindrical tower is made of metal lath covered in cement plaster. The lantern room and cast-iron railing were manufactured by the Champion Iron Works Company in Canton, Ohio.

A blueprint illustrating the Los Angeles Light Station site at the end of the San Pedro Breakwater. *Courtesy Eric Castro-Bran.*

The light to illuminate the port entry came from a fourth-order bivalve Fresnel lens. The hand-carved lens was manufactured in 1911 in Paris by Barbier, Bernard and Turenne, makers of many of the Fresnel lenses used around the world, which was constructed for the U.S. Lighthouse Service. It is unique in that it is last fourth-order to have a bivalve mercury float lens, in which the lens rotated on a basin filled with mercury.

The light station was established on March 1, 1913. The light was produced by an incandescent oil vapor lamp. The flash characteristic for the lens was a white flash every fifteen seconds. The light could be seen approximately twelve to fourteen miles.

Prior to electricity, a clockwork mechanism was used. It was wound by hand, and as the weights and pulleys descended, it caused the light to rotate and would create the flash sequence known to mariners.

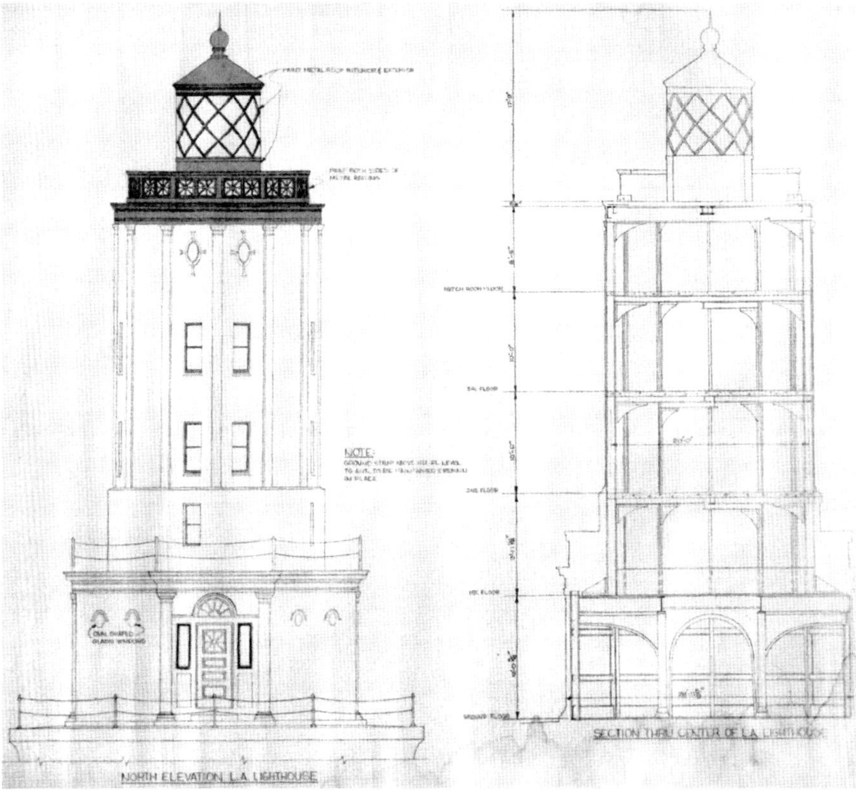

Blueprints of the Los Angeles Light Station, illustrating the ornate details of this one-of-a-kind lighthouse. *Courtesy Eric Castro-Bran.*

In 1932, the light source was changed from incandescent oil (kerosene) vapor to electricity and a translucent green cover was placed over the light source, producing a flashing green light to distinguish it from the surrounding white lights of the nearby terminals and refineries. Since then, the light has produced one green beam every fifteen seconds.

In 1935, a ball-bearing system was installed and the mercury float was removed. In addition, an electric motor replaced the clockwork mechanism.

The lighthouse was manned by lighthouse keepers and assistant keepers. The first keeper assigned was John Olson, who was aided by two assistant keepers. Since the lighthouse is located offshore and was not designated to accommodate families, its keepers were often separated from their families for weeks at a time.

Lighthouse Keeper Willard Miller served from 1915 to 1922. He was a veteran of the Spanish-American War and received the Congressional

Right: The lighthouse structure was painted all white, except for the lantern room, which had black trim, shortly after its completion in 1913. The tower stands seventy-three feet high. *Courtesy U.S. Coast Guard.*

Below: In 1918, the pilasters were painted black to improve the tower's visibility during periods of heavy fog. Also shown is the bridge to the boat landing. *Courtesy U.S. Coast Guard.*

A walkway/lookout tower was constructed around the upper portion of the tower and was removed in 1957. *Courtesy U.S. Coast Guard.*

Medal of Honor for his bravery at the Battle of Cienfuegos. Making great use of his time and available resources, Keeper Miller would routinely gather driftwood that washed up on shore and carve ornate music boxes and phonographs.

Many of the log entries in the keeper's log included: operated fog signal, painted and cleaned station, routine work, cleaned freshwater tank, installed new wick, cleaned lens and went to shore for mail and supplies.

In 1933, Long Beach experienced a magnitude 6.4 earthquake that abruptly shook the lighthouse. The mercury used to float the lens spilled out. Keeper Irving David Conklin, who served in the 1930s, did not report any significant damage to the tower.

One of Keeper Conklin's pet peeves was a visitor's question about taking a stroll on the breakwater. His response, according to a witness: "Did you ever stroll down a breakwater when twenty-foot seas are pounding over it? Try it sometime. They'll recover your body on a beach about week later."

The onset of World War II brought a new chapter to the history of the lighthouse. The U.S. Navy stepped in, and new construction began. This included a degaussing station, a radio direction–finding calibration unit and barracks for navy personnel.

Above: The *Point Judith*, an eighty-two-foot patrol boat, as seen here, is patrolling the San Pedro Bay where it arrived in 1966 and served for seven years in both law enforcement and search-and-rescue operations. *Courtesy U.S. Coast Guard.*

Right: A U.S. Coast Guard patrol boat with personnel approaching Los Angeles Light. *Courtesy U.S. Coast Guard.*

U.S. Coast Guard personnel arriving at Los Angeles Light with supplies for their stay. *Courtesy U.S. Coast Guard.*

In 1959, the two-tone foghorn known by locals as "Moaning Maggie" was replaced by a higher-pitched single-tone foghorn, referred to by locals as "Blatting Betty" and disliked by many local mariners.

The era of lighthouse keepers at the light came to an end when the Coast Guard automated the light in 1973. In November 1986, the Coast Guard concluded that with advances in solar technology available, it was possible to convert Los Angeles Light from generator power to solar power without a significant reduction in the visibility of the light. Any reduction would be offset by the addition of RACON, a radar transponder, to Los Angeles Approach Lighted Bell Buoy. In addition, an economic analysis surmised that solar power is the least costly and most efficient method of operating the light, especially as there were ongoing challenges with the batteries charging to full capacity.

U.S. Coast Guard helicopter flying over Point Vicente Lighthouse in Rancho Palos Verdes, circa 1960. *Courtesy U.S. Coast Guard.*

Postcard of San Pedro Harbor, Los Angeles. Circa 1900. *Author's collection.*

Front view of Point Fermin Lighthouse, San Pedro. *Courtesy Kim Castro-Bran.*

Mission San Buenaventura, Ventura. *Author's collection.*

A view of Main Street, Ventura, circa 1920. *Author's collection.*

Point Hueneme Lighthouse illuminating the entrance to the Hueneme Harbor. *Courtesy John M. Ambicki Jr.*

The *Bahama Star*, later renamed *La Jenelle*, in port. The ship would later meet a disastrous end on the rocks of the Ventura coast. *Author's collection.*

A cargo ship in the Port of Hueneme, the only deep-water port between Los Angeles and San Francisco. *Courtesy Kim Castro-Bran.*

The lantern room of the Point Hueneme Lighthouse with the new LED light. *Courtesy John M. Ambicki Jr.*

San Pedro, the annexed harbor to Los Angeles, circa late 1800s. *Author's collection.*

Ceremony aboard the USCGC *Conifer*, San Pedro, California. *Courtesy Eric Castro-Bran.*

USCGC *George Cobb* in its homeport of San Pedro, California. *Courtesy Kim Castro-Bran.*

Right: Sail boat participating in the Tall Ships Festival in San Pedro, with the Los Angeles Harbor Light (Angel's Gate) in the background. *Courtesy Kim Castro-Bran.*

Below: U.S. Naval Sea Cadets, Haven Division, are seen in drill formation in front of the visitors' center at the Point Vicente Lighthouse. *Courtesy Kim Castro-Bran.*

Left: Lynda Carter, starring as Wonder Woman, is seen prepping to film "The Bermuda Triangle Crisis," season 2, episode 4 at the lighthouse, which was referred to as Paradise Island in the episode. *Courtesy Point Vicente Lighthouse Collection.*

Below: Point Vicente lighthouse is one of the most breathtaking and photographed static objects on the Southern California coast. This photo shows the lighthouse with the prominent point and mature palm trees from the park area of the Point Vicente Interpretive Center. *Courtesy John M. Ambicki Jr.*

Right: Seen here is one of the dolphins with a trainer during one of the many shows at Marineland. Opening in 1954, Marineland delighted visitors until it closed its doors in 1987 after being purchased by Sea World. *Author's collection.*

Below: Fresnel lens inside the lantern room with views of the peninsula. *Courtesy John M. Ambicki Jr.*

View of the Palos Verdes Peninsula coastline, as seen from the Trump National Golf Club. *Courtesy Kim Castro-Bran.*

Iconic Arch Rock of the Channel Islands. *Courtesy Kim Castro-Bran.*

Above: Rock art of Chumash Native Americans in the Chumash Painted Cave, near Santa Barbara (not to be confused with Painted Cave in Santa Rosa, Channel Islands). *Courtesy Kim Castro-Bran.*

Right: Artwork of the Channel Islands National Park, depicting the abundant sea life and Arch Rock. *Courtesy Joel Anderson ©2015 Anderson Design Group, Inc. All rights reserved. www.ADGstore.com.*

Panoramic view of Lions Lighthouse for Sight with visitors surrounding lighthouse. *Courtesy Kim Castro-Bran.*

Captain Jerry Boylan, piloting the *Conception* to Santa Rosa Island. *Courtesy Kim Castro-Bran.*

The Parkers' Lighthouse restaurant, as seen in the foreground, with the Lions Lighthouse for Sight in the background. *Courtesy Kim Castro-Bran.*

A view of the *Queen Mary* in the Port of Long Beach. *Courtesy Kim Castro-Bran.*

Rainbow Pier, resembling a giant rainbow, was a breakwater with a roadway on its surface. It protected the auditorium, which had suffered from storms and coastal erosion. *Author's collection.*

U.S. battleships at anchor in the Port of Long Beach, 1936. *Author's collection.*

A postcard of Dead Man's Island in San Pedro. *Author's collection.*

The primary and auxiliary lenses of Long Beach Lighthouse. *Courtesy Kim Castro-Bran.*

Lions Lighthouse for Sight, located in Shoreline Aquatic Park in Long Beach. *Courtesy Kim Castro-Bran.*

Solar Power

Los Angeles Light was the first lighthouse in California to switch to solar power in February 1987 at a cost of $15,000. The fourth-order Fresnel lens at Los Angeles Harbor Lighthouse was surveyed to include retention as an artifact and licensing to a recognized historical society, museum or other federal agency.

In 1987, a new beacon replaced the Fresnel lens, and in 1988, the solar panels were relocated from the station-keeper building to the second level of the lighthouse, with an added support platform installed. Relocating the solar panels to a higher platform was an effort to increase the amount of sun absorption from a low solar charging rate. Fortunately, with improvements and reliability in solar panels over the years, the efficiency of the light source has remained constant.

Today, the modern lighthouse lens continues to be maintained by the Coast Guard Aids to Navigation Team Los Angeles–Long Beach, based at Terminal Island, and the light is operated by solar power.

It was concluded that the best place for the Fresnel lens was the Los Angeles Maritime Museum. The museum is a special facility of the

The entrance to U.S. Coast Guard Base Terminal Island, California, with personnel on duty at the guard shack. Circa 1960s. *Courtesy U.S. Coast Guard.*

Left: This fourth-order bivalve Fresnel lens is currently on display at the Los Angeles Maritime Museum. *Courtesy Kim Castro-Bran.*

Below: Los Angeles Maritime Museum, San Pedro, California. *Courtesy U.S. Coast Guard.*

city of Los Angeles Department of Recreation and Parks. The lens was temporarily housed in a warehouse before being transferred to the Maritime Museum. The lens is currently and beautifully showcased in the museum and affords easy access for visitors. For museum information, please visit lamaritimemuseum.org.

In 1992, a tugboat was renamed *Angel's Gate* and transferred to the museum. When in operation, the tug provides educational harbor tours for museum members and students, which include going by the lighthouse, located south of the museum.

When visitors step out the museum's backdoor to see the tug, they will also notice nearby Los Angeles' battleship USS *Iowa*, which is the only battleship museum on the West Coast.

USCGC *Conifer*

Following the merger of the Lighthouse Service and the Coast Guard in 1939, the Coast Guard revisited an earlier proposal put forth from the United States Lighthouse Service. The proposal was to help in maintaining lighthouse tenders, also referred to as offshore lighted ships, with delivery of equipment and supplies, as well as regular maintenance and upkeep. The solution proposed by the Lighthouse Service included a series of sketches depicting a newly designed ship whose main mission would be to access and service these aging tenders.

The Lighthouse Service specified in its submission that "the ships would need to be equipped with dual screws for maneuverability, a shallow draft for work in shoal water, and a diesel-electric plant for endurance and speed." This new modern vessel would need to fulfill all the requests from the Lighthouse Service and supporting military efforts. This was the genesis for the "general-purpose tenders."

The ships' abilities were far reaching, according to the ships' brochure. Further responsibilities included "transporting materials and personnel for defense works, firefighting, search and rescue (SAR), gasoline pipeline pipe laying, aiding in the construction of LORAN stations, weather observations, salvage operations, and icebreaking," in addition to "marking new wrecks, adjusting aids to mark special areas, and maintaining harbor protection such as submarine nets."

On July 11, 1986, the *Conifer* was assigned to its final homeport of San Pedro, California. The *Conifer*'s new area of responsibility spanned the

California coast from San Simeon Cove, near Hearst Castle, south to the Mexican border and offshore six hundred miles.

In the words of a *Conifer* crew member, "We maintain the aid systems for the Port of Los Angeles/Long Beach, the busiest commercial harbor and in San Diego Bay, homeport of the U.S. Navy's Third Fleet. We are responsible for 120 Coast Guard Buoys, and 11 environmental buoys operated by the National Weather Service. The largest offshore Coast Guard Buoys are 33 feet in diameter and 25 feet tall."

On the evening of May 18, 1989, the *Conifer* observed the light during morning. The skies on that evening were overcast with a light haze, and visibility was about ten nautical miles. The conclusion was that the new optics had resulted in no significant improvement. The Coast Guard's conclusion was to change the optics to a fifteen to twenty nominal-range light, which would increase visibility. The *Conifer*'s commanding officer, H.E. Blaney Jr., stated, "Although most mariners using Los Angeles and Long Beach harbors have the use of electronic navigation systems, the master cannot be comfortable until he sees the harbor entrance. I believe we owe him the simple courtesy of returning this comfort zone that had formerly been provided."

Four months later, the Coast Guard rear admiral received a letter from the Law Offices of Frank E. Gumbinger that stated:

> *Please correct the defective operation and total lack of operation of the Los Angeles Light/Horn at the entrance to the Los Angeles Harbor. The Light has not been operable for some time and with the increased fog in the area I believe that it is critical that you or such other appropriate individual/entity immediately restore the intensity and operational status of the Los Angeles Light.*
>
> *If the solar battery operation of the Light was an experiment I believe that it has failed and urge you/the appropriate individual or entity to immediately restore the intensity and operational reliability of the Los Angeles Light by again "plugging it in."*

Days following the receipt of letter, the Coast Guard submitted a work order requesting Los Angeles Light convert from solar power back to AC power. Per the work order: "This change is required to increase the range of the main light to better serve mariners." The hope was that an interim change to generator power would restore the light back to its needed intensity. Though problems persisted, fortunately, with the improvement of solar power, the Los Angeles Light has since been able to benefit from the sun's energy as a power source.

James S. Woodward, a classical Fresnel lens specialist who was uniquely trained under a U.S. Lighthouse Service lampist during his service in the Coast Guard, was brought in to repair one prism with a brass sheet using a technique called a "lampist's repair" in 2009. In addition, Woodward inspected, stabilized or repaired each of the 144 joints, while any other prisms that were deemed damaged beyond repair were left unchanged.

Cabrillo Beach Booster Club

While the light continued shining, the forces and elements of nature continued to wear down the lighthouse. By the late 1990s, it was apparent that the structure was in disrepair. Due to budget constraints and environmental issues, including lead paint, the Coast Guard was at odds about what could be done to remedy the situation. Local residents and politicians wanted something to be done about the deteriorating structure, which was an eyesore to everyone.

With the increase in port traffic, including cruise ships bringing tourists, improvements were needed. The Cabrillo Beach Booster Club stepped forward with a plan to renovate the historical structure. Working with the

Ray Olsen is seen working on the lighthouse floor, removing damaged planks. *Courtesy Tom Budar.*

Coast Guard and the City and Port of Los Angeles, the club applied for and received funding from the port to restore the lighthouse. The $1.8 million renovation began in October 2011. The structure received an extensive repair and renovation and was completed just in time to celebrate the lighthouse's centennial.

For information about visiting Los Angeles Harbor Light (Angel's Gate), please contact the Cabrillo Beach Booster Club by e-mail at cabrillobeachboosters@gmail.org. To contact the San Pedro Convention and Visitors Bureau, please visit SanPedroTourist.org.

Chapter 4

POINT VICENTE LIGHTHOUSE

The Palos Verdes Peninsula is the most prominent coastal feature between Point Loma to the south and Point Conception to the north, and as Captain George Vancouver continued to make his way down the Pacific Coast, it was impossible not to notice Palos Verdes, which he described as a "range of green trees."

On November 24, 1793, Vancouver named the area after his good friend Friar Padre Vincente de Santa Maria, of the nearby Mission of San Buenaventura. In July 1906, the U.S. Geographic Board officially changed the name to Point Vicente.

Shipmasters sailing these coastal waters between 1907 and 1909 submitted petitions requesting help to illuminate this jagged and dangerous stretch. In 1911, a whistle buoy was located off the nearby shores but was not sufficient.

The U.S. Lighthouse Service would later select the channel between the mainland coast and Catalina Island for a beacon, as it predicted it would become a major traffic zone for ships sailing up and down the coast to Los Angeles.

In 1914, the prominent point and roughly eleven-acre area was selected as the ideal site for a light station. The strategic beacon would help break up the long stretch of the Pacific Coast and also guide mariners away from the harsh cliffs and rocks. The area was so dangerous that the 1917 *Coast Pilot* advised mariners to keep away from the point.

The land, however, was already acquired. The owner was Frank Vanderlip Sr. Vanderlip, who was prominent in his own right. He served as the assistant secretary of the treasury under President McKinley during McKinley's second term, went on to a successful ten-year career as both the vice-president and president of National City Bank of New York and, after making his way out to California, turned to real estate acquisition and purchased the sixteen-thousand-acre Rancho de los Palos Verdes from the Bixby family in 1913.

Vanderlip, along with his land company, was not intimidated by the federal and local governments and was determined to keep his land stake. He was successful for five years—until 1920, when the United States attorney was in the process of entering a condemnation suit, threatening eminent domain. At that point, Vanderlip put forth an amicable offer. The offer was accepted, and all suits were dropped.

This was not the end of Frank Vanderlip Sr.'s legacy. In 1916, he built the Vanderlip estates near the Portuguese Bend area, along with his dream mansion. His vast contributions to the area granted him the title of "Father of Palos Verdes," along with the naming of Vanderlip Park in his honor.

The five-year tug-of-war trying to procure the property had no impact on commerce. In 1920, the Port of Los Angeles was on the fast track, passing San Francisco as the busiest port, with manufacturing, petroleum production and agriculture all on the rise. As a result, millions of dollars were being pumped into the local economy, and the West Coast was reaping all the benefits.

The proposal put forth for the light station would include the tower, quarters for both the keeper and assistant keeper with adequate accommodations for their families, a storage building, an oil house, piping for the water supply, a fog signal, fencing and a Fresnel lens.

Permission was finally granted to begin construction in July 1921, and all necessary filings were completed in 1922. The estimated cost for the project was $90,000, but Congress agreed to appropriate $80,000. The final cost, however, exceeded both the projected and approved costs: $102,871. Prior to the construction of the lighthouse, efforts were first made in the construction of the fog signal, which was put into operation on June 20, 1925.

The Light Station

Point Vicente lighthouse stands at the southwesternmost point of the Palos Verdes Peninsula in Rancho Palos Verdes and marks the northern end of the Catalina Channel on the Pacific Coast. It overlooks the San Pedro Channel from 185 feet above sea level. The light was lit on April 14, 1926.

Lighthouse keeper Anton Trittinger opens the front gate, welcoming visitors to the lighthouse grounds. Circa 1930s. *Courtesy Linda Cherney.*

It is a cylindrical-shaped, five-story, sixty-eight-foot-high tower and was constructed using plastered and reinforced concrete.

The pounding surf is 120.0 feet below the edge of the bluff. If you calculate another 10.0 feet for the rise from the edge to the base of the tower, plus 67.6 feet to the lights focal point, there would be 197.6 feet from sea level to focal plane.

A very similar lighthouse on the California coast would be Anacapa Lighthouse. One of the main differences between the two lighthouses is that Anacapa stands forty feet tall compared to Point Vicente's sixty-seven feet.

Three buildings were constructed alongside the lighthouse in 1924, providing housing for the keeper, the first and second assistant keepers and their families. The keeper's house is located near the center of the complex in a semicircular turnabout. It is a plain white, wood-frame, stucco, fifty-two- by forty-one-and-a-half-square-foot, two-story structure with a peak-shaped, Spanish red-tile roof. The ground floor consists of a den, living room, dining room and bathroom. The second floor contains four bedrooms and a bathroom.

Lighthouse blueprints designed by the U.S. Lighthouse Service, Eighteenth District, San Francisco. *Courtesy Eric Castro-Bran.*

The first and second assistant keepers' houses are both identical: plain white, wood-frame and stucco. However, they differ from the keepers' house, as they are rectangular twenty-nine- by sixty-eight-square-foot one-story structures, but they echo the design of the keeper's quarters with the same Spanish red-tile roofs. Undoubtedly, California's Spanish influence was instrumental in their design. The floor plan of each house consists of three bedrooms, a full bath, a living room, a dining room and a kitchen. All three houses contain full basements.

The foghorn building is large in scale at thirty-four by thirty-three square feet, and it is one large room with a smaller entry room on the side. In keeping with the station's architecture, this room, along with the rest of the buildings on the premises, maintained the red-tile roof and white stucco exterior.

The operations building, which was large in scale, consisted of two maintenance rooms, six administrative offices, one bathroom and a radio room. In addition, there was a transit barracks that was similar to a large

Right: The Spanish Revival–style architecture of Point Vicente Lighthouse is emphasized by the stark white column with black trim highlighting the iron cross-pattern, as seen in the windows. *Courtesy Linda Cherney*.

Below: Lighthouse grounds circa late 1920s. In a clockwise direction, the garage is in the foreground to the left. Directly behind is the two-story keeper's quarters. The fog signal station is seen in the background. The building closest to the flagpole is the machine shop, followed by the lighthouse and assistant keeper's quarters. *Courtesy Linda Cherney*.

The fog-signal building contained a large engine, a compressor and a tank of air. *Courtesy Linda Cherney.*

recreation room. These buildings were constructed in 1966 and located along the northeastern border of the complex. However, they were razed due to lead contamination.

The foghorn consisted of a ten-inch air whistle whose distinct, deep-throated sound was the only one of its kind on the Pacific Coast, and it was put into service on June 20, 1925. Full built-in workbenches with drawers were constructed for keeping tools and supplies.

The signature of the foghorn was a one-second blast, followed by two seconds of silence and then another blast followed by fifty-three seconds of silence. It operated using compressed air that emitted the sound and had two 4-foot- by 11-foot-9-inch receivers with a capacity of 150 cubic feet of air and used a Fairbanks Morse 4-cycle horizontal engine, built in 1907. Its sound was reportedly heard three miles out to sea and required sixty-five pounds of pressure in order to sound the whistle. The foghorn alone required on-duty personnel as the engine needed to be started by hand and would run on diesel fuel.

Lighthouse keeper Anton Trittinger, in full uniform, is seen climbing the elaborate, spiral staircase. *Courtesy Linda Cherney.*

In May 1971, the Coast Guard announced that "the old compressed-air fog horns at Point Vicente Lighthouse will be replaced with modern, more reliable electronic horns. The change is part of the Coast Guard's nationwide Lighthouse Automation and Modernization Program (LAMP) that will allow many stations to be automated and unmanned, thereby reducing operating costs without reduction in services."

As you enter the lighthouse tower, the stairway leading to the lantern room has a cast-iron spiral railing that ascends in a clockwise direction, guiding visitors up and around the seventy-nine stairs. There are three landings with window views on each floor. At the top of the stairs is the fifth floor, a glass-enclosed circular room at the top of the tower, where the Fresnel lens is housed.

Anton Trittinger (who is over six feet tall) is sitting inside the third-order Fresnel lens, polishing the 1,500-watt lamp. *Courtesy Linda Cherney.*

A steel door on the fifth floor leads outside to a catwalk. On the perimeter of the catwalk, there is a narrow walkway. This area circles the windows with views of the Fresnel lens from the outside looking in and breathtaking panoramic views facing outward. The northern side of the lantern room was originally painted black and later changed to white to prevent the light from bothering the neighbors.

The light is a third-order Fresnel lens and is encased in glass with steel framework holding the curved-glass panel. It emits a beam of light across a two-hundred-degree arc of coastline and water. The light flashes twice within a twenty-second period and has a total eclipse of nineteen seconds.

It was invented by Augustin-Jean Fresnel, built in Paris, France, and manufactured by Barbier, Bernard and Turenne, the oldest lens-making company in the world, in 1886.

It has been widely reported that the Fresnel lens was first shipped to Alaska and served there for forty years prior to arriving at Point Vicente. These reports were published as early as the 1950s if not even earlier. However, they have not been able to be substantiated, and there are no records of any lighthouses in Alaska that show such a transfer.

What is known is that the lens arrived at the station in late to early 1925 or 1926 most likely directly from France. The glass is ground into prisms and weighs in the area of 1,200 pounds. The prisms are held in place by a cast-brass frame. Each prism is positioned precisely in the direction of the traveling light beam and is rotated by a small motor at its base. Once electrified, it was a 1,500-watt bulb that enabled the light to be seen approximately twenty miles out to sea, and some have reported seeing the light just over twenty miles away. In 1993, the 1,500-watt lamp was replaced by a 1,000-watt lamp with only slight impact on projection.

The lens rotates once every forty seconds, is double sided and has two ten-inch bull's-eyes. The mariner sees it flash two times every twenty seconds. When the one-thousand-watt bulb is combined with the massive lens, the intensity of the light is rated at 2.1 million candlepower. The lens rotates using a compact motor located below the lens and only using one-twelfth horsepower.

There are seven buildings associated with the lighthouse. The grounds at Point Vicente are much the way they were in 1926 when the light was built and the only road to San Pedro, six and a half miles away, was gravel. The keeper's quarters are currently used as Coast Guard housing.

Lighthouse Keepers

For the first thirteen years of service, the lighthouse was operated and maintained by the United States Lighthouse Service. There were only three head keepers in Point Vicente's history. George W. L'Hommedieu was transferred from Mile Rocks Lighthouse near San Francisco to become Point Vicente's first head keeper in 1926. George was joined by his first assistant keeper, Harry Davis, and his second assistant keeper, Ben South. Quickly, the common cordial relations between the three keepers, as well as among their families, descended into bitter feuds.

As allegations and charges were being filed, assistant superintendent F.J. Otter was brought in to assess the situation. He determined in his report: "There has been considerable friction at Point Vicente Light Station between the keeper and his two assistants for some time, and while some of the charges are of a serious nature, there are many of them of a petty nature and found to be considerably magnified. It is known that the Keeper has at times a violent temper which might be overlooked by an assistant of proper temperament." The report further added, "Mrs. L'Hommedieu, the wife of the Keeper, interjects herself into the Government affairs and has caused a considerable amount of the trouble at the Station."

The keeper was credited in the report for the well-kept grounds, but due to the volatility of the relationships, it was concluded, "Friction will always arise at this Station at intervals due to the ill feelings between the Keeper and Assistants, and particularly their wives." All three keepers were reprimanded, and Keeper L'Hommedieu was transferred to Piedras Blanca's Lighthouse.

A new "by-the-book" head keeper by the name of Anton Trittinger, with plenty of lighthouse experience, arrived at the station. Though widely reported that Trittinger arrived at the station in 1930, relatives of the keeper actually report that the keeper arrived in 1929 (perhaps even 1928). His earlier arrival may have been a response to the simultaneous departure of the head keeper and his two assistants.

Anton Trittinger was born in Vienna, Austria, in May 1892 and is noted for his meticulous attention to detail. A March 15, 1935 article in the *Los Angeles Times* stated, "For the third straight year the Point Vicente Lighthouse, flashing warnings to mariners on the tip end of the knob of land which swerves into the ocean between San Pedro and Redondo, has received this honor."

The prestigious award the paper was referring to is the Lighthouse Efficiency Award. The article continues, "The efficiency flag, which designated the lighthouse reservation as the most efficient and best

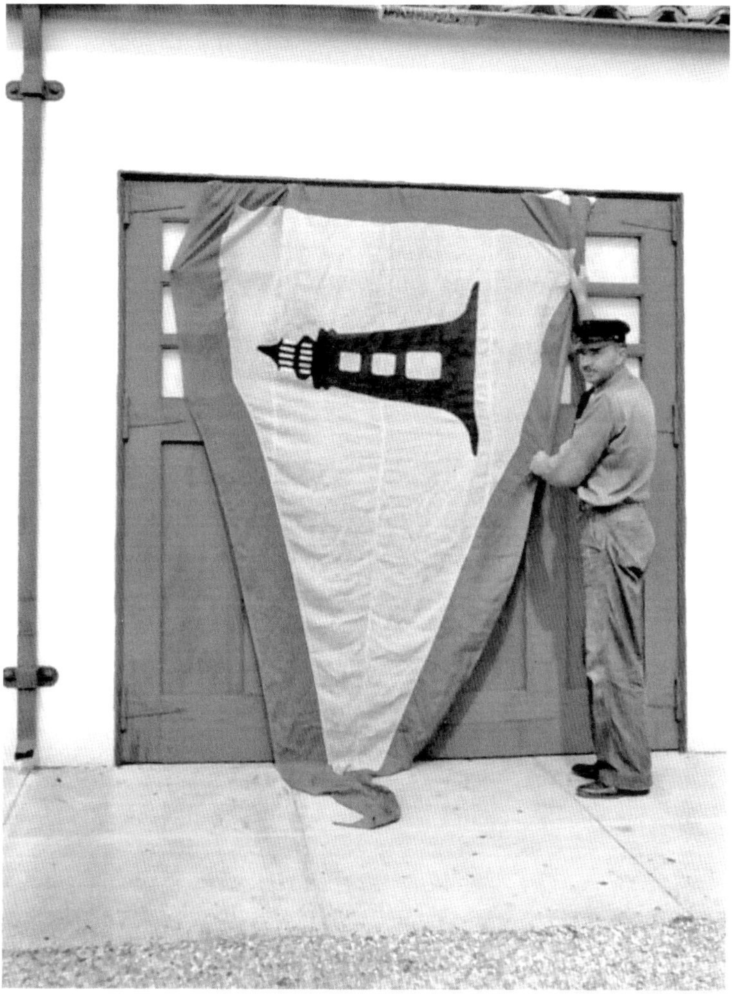

Head keeper Anton Trittinger is shown displaying the "District Efficiency Pennant Award" over the double doors of the fog signal building in 1935. *Courtesy Linda Cherney.*

maintained in the district, yesterday was in the hands of Anton Trittinger, head keeper of the light."

Trittinger lived at the station with his wife, Frieda, and their two daughters, Mary and Sophie. The daughters were only two years apart, and the spacious grounds were their playground. Soon the daughters would have playmates, as the first assistant keeper, T.A. Atkinson, arrived at the station with his wife and four young children in 1931.

Anton Trittinger is seen with his wife, Frieda, and their two daughters, Mary and Sophie, in front of the keeper's quarters in the early 1930s. *Courtesy Linda Cherney.*

Mary and Sophie grew up at the station as their father served over fifteen years as head keeper. The fun was also balanced with chores and work with everyone pitching in. Anton Trittinger was fair but also strict—understandably so, as some areas of the compound initially were unfenced and posed many hazards for young children.

In 1939, as the U.S. Lighthouse Service was absorbed by the Coast Guard, all lighthouse personnel were given the option to enlist as military members of the Coast Guard or work as civilians. In addition to continuing his position as head keeper of the station, Anton Trittinger also joined the Coast Guard. He left the station in 1945, and in addition to his outstanding service, he is also notably remembered as the longest-serving lighthouse keeper at the station.

A third and final keeper, Joe May, arrived at the station in 1945. Joe had accepted his position at Point Vicente following his tenure at Anacapa Lighthouse and was sixty years old when he arrived at the station.

In 1941, movie actress Lana Turner visited the lighthouse grounds for a promotional movie tour. She is seen posing with Anton Trittinger. *Courtesy Linda Cherney and MGM.*

Frieda Trittinger is seen sweeping the walkway outside the keeper's home. The family cared for three acres of geraniums, which are seen in full bloom around the fountain. *Courtesy Linda Cherney.*

Joe May (center) in his Lighthouse Service civilian uniform. To the left of May is George Livesey, and an unidentified serviceman is to his right. *Courtesy U.S. Coast Guard.*

As the two lighthouses are very similar (except that Point Vicente stands much taller than Anacapa), it was an easy transition for Joe, with one added bonus: he was now surrounded by palm trees and an accessible road as opposed to waiting for a boat to leave the island.

In following the tradition of Anton Trittinger, Joe kept the lighthouse grounds "spotless," as they were often described, and he served ten years at the station. When Joe left the station in 1955, it signaled the end of an era, as Point Vicente said good-bye to its last official lighthouse keeper.

As Joe gave his parting words at his retirement ceremony, he stood proudly, clutched his keeper's hat, looked down and caressed one of the gold braids that was part of the Lighthouse Service emblem. He then took a moment and reflected on his service.

He commented that the service "dates back to the old Boston light in the days of the Massachusetts commonwealth." Joe was talking about the first lighthouse in America's history, Boston Lighthouse on Little Brewster Island. He mentioned that despite the fact that the lighthouse was destroyed during the Revolutionary War, it was proudly rebuilt in 1783 and still stands. He further added, "Aren't too many of us left. Only me and George Ward at Port Hueneme in the Eleventh Coast Guard District. And come next Thursday, there'll be only George."

During and After World War II

It was during this time that California's defense industry started to see an immediate boom with not only aircraft and ship construction on the rise but also a surge in government contracts and immediate procurement and construction of military installations throughout the area. Unemployment fell to an all-time low, and as word spread of economic growth, many flocked to California in pursuit of patriotism and opportunities. An open border with Mexico allotted for workers to assist in wartime efforts.

Of all metropolitan areas, Los Angeles would take first place with the largest amount of growth. It's mass oil and mineral resources helped aid in this growth running at maximum production. New industry was on the rise for California, and alongside the growth of the automobile, navigation into Los Angeles and Long Beach would be on a rapid incline.

During World War II, the peninsula was guarded by heavy fortified weapon emplacements at nearby Fort MacArthur. Caves were dug into the cliff to serve as lookouts. Like the other area lighthouses, Point Vicente would also dim its light for security. The wattage of the light was lowered to a mere twenty-five-watt lamp, and blackout curtains were hung over the windows in an effort to not aid any potential enemy vessels.

In 1943, on the other side of Palos Verdes Drive, the army put two large artillery guns up on the hill that guarded the port approaches to Los Angeles/Long Beach.

After World War II, the windows facing the communities behind the lighthouse were painted white to reduce the white light that continually

An aerial view of the lighthouse compound, showing Palos Verdes Drive West and the surrounding undeveloped land in the late 1950s to early 1960s. *Courtesy U.S. Coast Guard.*

Light Station Crew: Boatswain's Mate Chief Petty Officer Arthur W. Gename front, center, with Melvin W. Dickinson EN3 to his right and Thomas L. Reece SA to his left, with "security dog" Pesty. Radio Station personnel in background: In front of door Chief Radio Electrician and Commanding Officer (CHRELE) Charles A. Hatfield on left and CHRELE Executive Officer Thomas H. Renfroe on right with radio station crew, 1964. *Courtesy Point Vicente Lighthouse Collection.*

reflected on the surrounding houses. Now as the light rotates, the full force of the light is only directed to the sea.

Beginning in the early 1950s, the Coast Guard put into operation the HO4S-1G and 2G helicopter models. The two-deck helicopters were used in search-and-rescue operations and the proximity of the helo pad at the lighthouse made it a convenient landing site and a base for many sea rescue operations.

That same year, the air force built Nike Missile Site #55 on the hill, including an underground tunnel about one hundred yards in length through the hill. The site was self-contained with everything needed to live, work and operate the missiles. When the site was dismantled, the City of Rancho Palos Verdes was able to utilize the main building and turned it into city hall, with the Coast Guard maintaining the rest of the property.

The radio station was built in 1934 and is sixteen by twenty-four feet square with two rooms originally. It was one of only five manned stations. The radio station served as the main radio station for Southern California. The station had the primary responsibility for monitoring radio distress frequencies and relaying assistance calls to the Rescue Coordination Center in Long Beach.

Coast Guardsmen on duty at the radio station were constantly receiving and transmitting information around the clock. Four radiomen were on

A Coast Guardsman on duty at the radio station. *Courtesy Eric Castro-Bran.*

A Sikorsky helicopter is shown as it landed on the designated helo pad at the lighthouse. *Courtesy U.S. Coast Guard.*

duty twenty-four hours a day, with one man on watch all the time at the lighthouse. Additionally, they were responsible for monitoring five various frequencies constantly. In addition to maritime traffic, the radio installation also played a key role in aviation and defense communications for the Eleventh Coast Guard district. Today, a fence circles the entire light station for protection from the jagged cliffs and the rock beach below.

Every half hour there would be a silent period that lasted for three minutes. It was during this time that all hands would listen for any distress calls that may have gone unnoticed before. No ship-to-shore calls were made during this time as well.

The radio room was originally located in the building that housed the carpenter shop, which today is the keeper's office. It was relocated to the former barracks building.

The lighthouse was manned until 1971, when automated equipment and remote control operators took over its operation, and the radio station was officially closed with a decommissioning ceremony on May 1, 1980.

SS *Dominator*

Many ships have met tragedy and turmoil in these waters, but none was as prominent as the SS *Dominator*. On March 13, 1961, the Greek World War II freighter was carrying 10,200 tons of wheat from Portland, Oregon, embarking on a long voyage to Algiers, located on the west side of a bay of the Mediterranean Sea. As evening was approaching, the ship was only eight miles away from Long Beach harbor, but due to a combination of navigational error, harsh elements and heavy sea fog, visibility was poor, and in a moment's notice, the ship slammed into a rock reef one hundred yards off Rocky Point, at the point between Lunada Bay and Malaga Cove.

Captain Papanicolopoulos radioed in for assistance on the ships emergency radio, which was a Morse code key-type of communication and gave his location in the proximity of Long Beach Harbor. This was to be one of many errors. The captain then refused either Coast Guard or tugboat aid, fearing potential financial expenses. As water was seeping into multiple areas of the ship, the captain still declined to heed any advice and believed that the sheer water power from high tide would be enough to propel the ship back to sea. This may have been plausible if not for the considerable amount damage to the hull. In normal conditions, the loaded ship would require about twenty-seven feet of water to float. It was days later when the captain finally relented and requested assistance. The ship had finally settled with a sharp fifteen-degree list to starboard.

The ship and its cargo were insured for just over $1 million, and only fifteen days following the wreck, both were already up for auction. The final bid for the ship was just over $16,000, while the wheat sold for $75,000 cash. On the five-mile boat ride from Redondo Beach to the *Dominator*, the new owners commented that it looked as big as the *Queen Mary*, but they soon realized it had all the trappings of a "dead ship," with the sounds of creaking and moaning rising from the hull. A bitter feud broke out between the owner of the ship and the owner of the wheat. It was supposed to take one month to remove the wheat, but instead, it took four. The prolonged unloading of the wheat angered the owner of the ship, as his goal was to try to refloat the ship quickly. Following many threats and gun violence, the Coast Guard was brought in to observe and ease tensions, and in the end, the wheat owners made a profit of over $100,000, while the ship's owner walked away with a deficit and was also charged by the wheat owners of purposely dumping fuel, resulting in a three-year probationary sentence. The ship's owner stated, "The new lesson after all this was, 'Don't buy a ship to salvage unless you buy the cargo, too.'"

"The Hollywood Lighthouse"

Hollywood film studios would soon take notice of this ideal filming locale, with requests continually coming in for both television and movies. All of the area lighthouses had movie rosters of their own, but undoubtedly, Point Vicente, dubbed the "Hollywood Lighthouse," is center stage.

Olivia Newton-John seen at Terminal Island Base singing her hit song "I Honestly Love You." *Courtesy Eric Castro-Bran.*

In 1998, Olivia Newton John filmed a music video here, a re-recording of her iconic song from the 1970s "I Honestly Love You." The museum was transformed into a living room setting for one scene, and Olivia sang as she climbed the lighthouse stairs, circled around the lens and walked outside onto the catwalk. As the sunlight dimmed, she was surrounded by the illuminating light and the feeling of nostalgia and love.

In 2001, the movie *Pearl Harbor*, starring Ben Affleck and Kate Beckinsale and directed by Jerry Bruckheimer, was also filmed at the lighthouse. The movie depicted the surprise Japanese air raid on Pearl Harbor. The hospital scene was filmed in the lighthouse museum, and other scenes were shot on the lighthouse grounds. In addition, countless movie and television shows, both local and foreign, have used the lighthouse and its grounds as a backdrop.

National Register

On November 17, 1979, the lighthouse was added to the National Register of Historic Places, and one month later, dedication ceremonies took place to commemorate the occasion. The ceremonies were planned by the Rancho de los Palos Verdes Historical Society.

Rear Admiral H.W. Parker presided over the ceremonies and commented:

> *For those of you who have been to sea, I know you agree with me that there is nothing more reassuring when returning from a long voyage than seeing your lighthouse flashing her familiar characteristics, or if in fog, hearing the mournful cry of her fog signal. Lights such as this guard the headland of the world. But nowhere more efficiently than here in our beloved United States, where young Coastguardsmen, such as those stationed here do their duty. These lights are all electrified now but not too many years ago they burned oil in their wicks. That's where even today we affectionately refer to our men stationed at lighthouses as "Wickies."*
>
> *This tribute to you and the members of the Historical Society pay to this beautifully kept and very important lighthouse on the Pacific Coast is well placed. We appreciate the honor you are bestowing upon us through this unselfish act.*

The Ghost

Even when the weather is stormy, there is an alluring beauty about the lighthouse. The lighthouse is like no other in Southern California. There is a cold, damp feeling when you enter the steel door into the lighthouse and the saltwater smell of being on a large ship at sea. The height of the lighthouse is put in proportion as your head folds back to take in the substantial spiral staircase. The only thing needed is the quintessential ghost story, consisting of chains and eerie noises, which this lighthouse has had for decades.

It started when one keeper spotted a strange apparition at nightfall of a woman in a flowing white gown frantically pacing the tower, seemingly searching for her love lost at sea. Another story says a keeper wandered off the cliff one night and fell to his death off the rocky beach, while still others proclaim that it was not the keeper but rather his wife who fell to her death.

This ghostly rumor, however, was debunked by an assistant who worked on the premises when he discovered that the ghostly apparition was an unusual reflection created by the light as it rotated. Others attributed the apparition to the paint on the windows. Originally, the layer of paint was much thinner, and when observing the lighthouse from the hill, the light would rotate and cast a ghostly shadow on the window.

Lighthouse Support Team

In 1992, the U.S. Coast Guard sent a "want ad" to the U.S. Coast Guard Auxiliary looking for a few good auxiliarists. The ad stated, "We need a dedicated leader and a couple of helpers to perform the duties of lighthouse guide for Point Vicente Light. A love for lighthouses is a plus. This individual would need to keep the light looking shipshape as well as other duties."

Eric Castro-Bran, an auxiliarist who was also working with the Coast Guard's Aids to Navigation Team (ANT), volunteered to take on this project. His mechanical and electrical background, as well as his certification as a technician with the ANT, enabled him to expand his duties to repairing machinery and electrical issues and servicing the Fresnel lens. In addition to this, he and the auxiliary team mowed the lawns and maintained the grounds. He also worked to convert the old fog signal building into the current visitors' center. Castro-Bran was joined

Eric Castro-Bran, pictured in his auxiliary uniform, poses in front of the lighthouse. *Author's collection.*

by a handful of volunteers from his flotilla. In opening the lighthouse grounds to school tours, special events and regular monthly open houses, Castro-Bran and his fellow auxiliary members have welcomed over 300,000 visitors since 1992. The Coast Guard Auxiliary has by special appointment named him "lighthouse keeper."

Point Vicente Interpretive Center

Within walking distance of the lighthouse is the Point Vicente Interpretive Center. The center originally opened in 1984 and, after a full renovation and expansion of almost ten thousand square feet, reopened its doors in the summer of 2006. The area has been described as the best cliff-top whale-watching stop in the Los Angeles area.

From December through April, a group of dedicated volunteers, sponsored by the Los Angeles Chapter of the American Cetacean Society and the Cabrillo Marine Aquarium, keep watch and tally the gray whale population as it begins its migration to the warmer temperatures of Baja California, Mexico. The caravan of whales along the coast of western North America starts every year like clockwork in the winter and continues into the spring. Leading the pack are the expectant-mother whales as they leave the cold Arctic temperatures, giving birth along the way in the warmer coastal lagoons. These volunteers and onlookers get to witness the longest whale migration on the planet.

In addition to the whale watching and scenic panorama views, the center is a regional museum and focuses on the natural and cultural history of the Palos Verdes Peninsula and adjacent waters. It offers interactive and static exhibits, giving both kids and adults an educational and fun experience.

The Point Vicente Interpretive Center (PVIC) is located adjacent to the Point Vicente Lighthouse at 31501 Palos Verdes Drive West, Rancho Palos Verdes. *Courtesy Kim Castro-Bran.*

The excessive amount of heat energy emitted from the Fresnel lens is so constant and intense that it has started to buckle the floor area below the lens and has also caused the paint to peel above the lens surface. A new, more efficient LED light is destined to take its place, and the Point Vicente Interpretive Center is projected to be the future home of the lighthouse's Fresnel lens. The location offers more visibility and access for visitors to this 1800s gem.

The lighthouse would be fully manned until 1971. This was the year when the lighthouse would be automated by a remote electronic aids-to-navigation monitoring system. Inside the base of the lighthouse tower is the electrical power supply for the light. The electric boxes mounted on the wall provide all the power that is needed for the light. When the electricity fails, auxiliary batteries take over until power is restored. There are separate electrical cables that run from the batteries to the light in the top of the tower.

To this day, the Coast Guard Aids to Navigation Team Los Angeles/Long Beach (CG ANT LA/LB), in addition to many other duties, continues to make sure that the light is well lit for mariners.

U.S. Naval Sea Cadets

The U.S. Naval Sea Cadet Corps (USNSCC) Haven Division signed on in October 1997 to assist with monthly open houses and special events. As the grounds of the lighthouse compound are spacious, the cadets have been quintessential in keeping order and structure with the large numbers of arriving visitors.

Founded in 1958 by the Navy League of the United States under the direction of the Department of the Navy, the cadets are supported by both the U.S. Navy and Coast Guard. Among other roles, they have been instrumental in assisting with gate access (signing in and informing visitors of rules), lighthouse and museum access, guiding visitors along designated paths, perimeter sentry, clean up and so forth. Following their duties, they also routinely practice their drills or go over protocol. Cadets range in age from thirteen through seventeen, and there is also a junior program for ages eleven through thirteen.

THE LIGHTHOUSE TODAY

It is located at 31555 Palos Verdes Drive in the city of Rancho Palos Verdes. When driving to the lighthouse station, there are two ways to enter the station. One is to approach it in a northwesterly direction, and the other is from the south, coming from where Marineland once stood, where today the Terranea Resort and Spa are located, only minutes away from the lighthouse.

Drivers will quickly see the caps of over four dozen royal palm trees dotting the Point Vicente Lighthouse Station. The lighthouse is nestled toward the rear right of the station and, from this angle, even though it stands sixty-seven feet tall, is many times hidden from view. But the number of palm trees elegantly arranged on the almost thirteen acres of grounds is sure to catch the attention of drivers. Coming from the south, there is only a quick left-turn lane, which is easy to miss. Once the oncoming traffic is clear, drivers can turn left onto the road and then proceed to a fork, where they can make an immediate left to lighthouse or continue straight to the Point Vicente Interpretive Center. Parking for the lighthouse, however, is in a dirt lot just outside lighthouse grounds. The Interpretive Center was recently renovated and has plenty of parking on its grounds. The great part about visiting this lighthouse is that the Interpretive Center is a nice complement to the lighthouse for a sightseeing tour and vice versa.

When you approach the lighthouse from the north (heading in a southwesterly direction), the lighthouse is somewhat more visible, but it is best to follow the sign from this direction that leads you to the Interpretive Center, as the entrance to both sites is from the same turnout. Google the Interpretive Center for directions rather than the lighthouse as directions given are more detailed, and visit www.vicentelight.org for dates and times.

The lighthouse is situated just over seventeen nautical miles from Catalina, thirty-seven from Santa Barbara, twenty-four from Malibu and almost fourteen from the Los Angeles International Airport, making it a very attractive tourist destination, with thousands of visitors arriving annually.

The harsh elements of endless wind, sea-salted air, time, earthquakes and age have slowly started to take a toll on the once "spit and polish" lighthouse. However, despite all this, it is an operational lighthouse and remains an important aid to navigation.

For ships leaving the harbors of Los Angeles and Long Beach, Point Vicente is the second beacon they see as they head up the coast or out to sea. If you are coming out of the Port of Long Beach, Long Beach light (Queen's Gate) is the first light you will see. If you are coming out of the Port of Los Angeles, you will see the Los Angeles Harbor Lighthouse (Angel's Gate Lighthouse).

Chapter 5

ANACAPA LIGHT STATION

The native Chumash called Anacapa *Anyapakh* or *Eneepaha*, meaning "ever changing" or "mirage." Their description of this volcanic island could not be more fitting, as the island has morphed over the course of millions of years, and the amount of land exposed or hidden has been reflective of the changing sea levels and tides. This, coupled with the heavy sea fog that is known to quickly descend on the area, makes the island seem to appear or disappear like a mirage.

As remote as this small island seems, it is only twelve miles from the mainland and is composed of a five-mile-long stretch of rock that is broken up into three small islets: East Island, Middle Island and West Island. It has a total landmass of just over one square mile and is located on the southern side of the eastern end of the Channel Islands.

The islands of San Miguel, Santa Rosa, Santa Cruz and Anacapa were once joined as a single island called Santarosae—that is, until sea levels increased again, giving us the four distinct islands that we know today. Archaeological sites show evidence of used abalone, mussel and limpet shells, indicating that the Chumash frequented Anacapa as a stopover to and from the mainland.

Anacapa was discovered by Juan Rodríguez Cabrillo in 1542 and by Spanish explorer De Portola in 1769, who named the island Las Mesitas, meaning "little tables." Later that year, Captain George Vancouver would give it the name as we know it by today, Anacapa, a derivative of its original Chumash name.

Vessels traveling to San Francisco along the west coast of Central and South America have been warned to watch out for or stay clear of this narrow passage, which may be camouflaged by a blanket of fog and without warning suddenly spring out from the depths of the sea. It was tempting to avoid it all together, but the risk was often necessary in an effort to save time.

On December 2, 1853, the *Winfield Scott*, a passenger steamship loaded with 450 passengers and crew members, as well as $1 million in gold, left San Francisco for Panama. The fog shielded the islands from view, tricking the captain into believing he was already clear of them. At full speed, the *Winfield Scott* crashed into a large rock off Middle Anacapa. Fortunately, all 450 on board survived, but the ship was lost. Today, the ship rests underwater and is part of the Channel Islands National Park and Marine Sanctuary and is listed on the National Register of Historic Places.

Following the wreck, President Franklin Pierce signed an executive order that designated Anacapa Island for lighthouse purposes. The U.S. Coast Survey Agency was sent out to assess the island in 1854 and concluded, "It is inconceivable for a lighthouse to be constructed on this mass of volcanic rock, perpendicular on every face, with an ascent inaccessible by any natural means." As a result, in 1874, Congress would fund Point Hueneme Lighthouse across the channel.

Illuminating the Island

In 1911, Congress allocated funds for an automatic acetylene beacon mounted on a fifty-foot metal tower at the eastern edge of Anacapa. A whistling buoy was also anchored about a half mile offshore. On February 28, 1921, the tank steamer *Liebre* was grounded on the east end of Anacapa, directly under the light tower. The wreck highlighted the inefficiency of the light during heavy fog, as well as the absence of a fog signal on the island.

Finally, in 1928, the Bureau of Lighthouses allotted funds to build a fully staffed lighthouse with support buildings. A cove construction was first on the agenda, as it would enable crews and supplies to gain access to the island. In December 1930, Carpenter Brothers of Beverly Hills, California, began construction and installed two crane hoists or "derricks," which were built into the landing cave area and powered by gasoline engines.

The lower crane was situated fifty-five feet above water level and hoisted cargo from incoming vessels onto the island's lower landing deck. The crane's

These derricks were used for lifting and transporting supplies, vehicles, boats, building materials and other cargo that needed to be moved on or off the island. *Courtesy Jerry Boylan.*

In this September 15, 1956 photo, newborn Leo Whaley III is held by his parents as they are transported to the island via the cargo box. *Courtesy Jerry Boylan.*

Spanish Revival–style residences constructed in 1932, with the lighthouse in the background. Three of the residences were subsequently razed. *Courtesy Jerry Boylan.*

The lighthouse is located on the highest point of East Anacapa. *Courtesy U.S. Coast Guard.*

boom was approximately forty feet long and carried a maximum load of five tons. An upper crane was located at the top landing of the stairway, and this crane would lift up to four tons with its fifty-foot boom and raise materials from the lower deck.

In 1931, the landing cove was completed, which included a docking area, a lower landing platform, a seawall, two cranes with crane houses and a stairway connecting these upper and lower levels. The lower crane was eventually removed.

Due to the complexity of the location, construction was organized in two phases. The first phase would allot for the landing facilities and roads, which were needed first before construction could begin for a lighthouse. The

Coast Guard personnel seen walking on the dirt road that leads to the main door of the Anacapa lighthouse. *Courtesy Kim Castro-Bran.*

second phase was for the construction of the tower and support buildings. In mid-1931, the Los Angeles–based M.W. Lippman construction company began building the lighthouse facilities.

On March 25, 1932, at a cost of $110,490, construction was completed, and the forty-four-foot lighthouse and its outlying buildings were put into service. The lighthouse is a cylindrical-shaped lighthouse constructed of brick and reinforced concrete. Similar to Point Vicente Lighthouse but shorter, it, too, emphasizes the Spanish Revival style of architecture. The light tower housed a third-order Fresnel lens that lit up the surrounding waters with a projection of over twenty miles out to sea.

The station would be equipped with a foghorn service, plus weather and radio monitoring. The first head keeper was Frederick S. Cobb, who would only serve one year on the island. Charles Coursey, who started as a second assistant keeper, was promoted to principal keeper in 1935 and served about five years at the station. Joseph "Joe" May arrived in 1938 and served eight years as head keeper until he was transferred to Point Vicente Lighthouse.

As Margaret Anderson, daughter of Assistant Keeper Leo Kellogg, remembered, "The keepers were always so busy on the island there was never any time to be bored. There was always so much to do."

The families used one truck on the island to haul groceries and supplies. Gravel roads took them to the landing, machine shop, lighthouse and out to where the current camping area is today. The families would also often get together to share meals and tell stories.

The dangers of the island were many, and when a boating mishap pinned Leo Kellogg's leg as he and Coast Guard crew members were lifting and hoisting a boat, the injury resulted in continuous knee pain for the assistant keeper. Following the accident, Kellogg was transferred to Point Arguello, followed by Point Hueneme Light Station, his final station.

Arch Rock is an iconic landmark of Anacapa and the Channel Islands National Park. It rises forty feet above the surface of the water and creates what looks like a rainbow-shaped rock, which some small boats like to pass through. Subjected to the bombardment of the elements, this natural feature will last as long as Mother Nature allows.

The service building, power house, fuel tanks and oil house were all close to one another. The oil house contained three two-thousand-gallon tanks of fuel. The power house, located above the fuel tanks, contained the generator and the radio room. In the 1980s, the power house was converted into apartments.

Water tanks were constructed to house fresh water, but vandals used the water tanks as target practice, thus ruining the water supply. The Coast

Right: Keeper Leo Kellogg sits on steps holding Skippy, his dog, and a cat. He served as assistant keeper from 1937 to 1940. *Courtesy Margaret Kellogg-Anderson.*

Below, from left to right: Leo Kellogg, Howard Fawcett, George Livesey (rear) and Joe May, digging a large trench on the island. *Courtesy Margaret Kellogg-Anderson.*

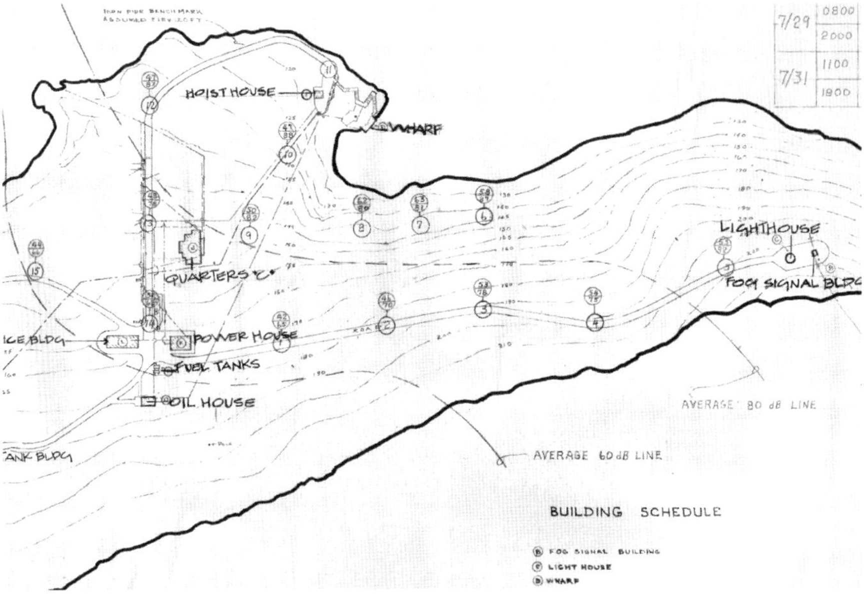

A chart of the islands with designated structures. *Author's collection.*

Guard came up with an ingenious solution to design the façade of the water tank building to look like a church. The idea worked, and the shooting ceased. In addition, the church-like structure kept rodents out and provided an added barrier of protection from the elements.

On April 26, 1938, President Franklin D. Roosevelt established Anacapa and Santa Barbara Islands as the Channel Islands National Monument. To further protect the islands and surrounding marine life, a one-mile area around the islands was also included. In 1980, the Channel Islands National Park was created and includes the five islands of Anacapa, Santa Cruz, Santa Rosa, Santa Barbara and San Miguel. The Channel Islands National Marine Sanctuary overlaps the Park boundary and encompasses about 1,200 square miles of ocean area within its boundaries.

Like the other area lighthouses, during World War II, Anacapa's light was extinguished, and its facilities became a coastal lookout station for the U.S. Navy, as the navy took over control of the Coast Guard during the war.

The Hermits

The four Coast Guard families who lived on the island in the 1930s were not alone. They had the company of two hermits. One of the hermits was called Charlie or "Anacapa Charlie." His full name was Charles Johnson, and he was described by Margaret Anderson, the daughter of Keeper Leo Kellogg, as "friendly, very well read and good looking." She also stated, "Charlie also had his is own home on the island." How or why Charlie was on the island was a mystery, and as much as he liked solitude, he also prided himself on keeping up on current events before everyone else. He was an avid fisherman, served as a steamship skipper on the Great Lakes and was a veteran of the Spanish-American War. Charlie arrived on the island in 1931, and upon his death eight years later, a Coast Guard cutter was sent to retrieve his body.

The most famous hermit of all was Raymond "Frenchy" LaDreau, whose French origins gave him his nickname. Frenchy lived on the island for twenty-eight years, mainly in the area of East Fish Camp. In his honor, Frenchy's Cove was named after him.

U.S. Coast Guard Arrive on the Island

From the early 1930s into the early 1960s, the Coast Guard manned the station lighthouse, which would include the lighthouse tower, lens and fog signal and a radio tower. Crews were also tasked with monitoring weather and radar, including reports.

Larry Boylan was the officer in charge, Boatswain Mate First Class with the United States Coast Guard, when he and his wife, Lois, arrived at Anacapa Island in the mid-1950s. Among other duties, Boylan was put in charge of the lighthouse. Their two children, Vicky and Jerry, would grow up on the island for about three years, knowing it as their playground. The island instilled in the children a sense of wonder and adventure, and the surrounding ocean gave them an unwavering respect for the sea. Young Jerry and Vicky would spend hours playing, splashing in the water and discovering the island.

Three years on the island and lighthouse keeping would prepare the Boylan family for their next relocation to Point Conception Lighthouse, followed by East Brother Light Station, and on to Texas, for yet another lighthouse duty station.

CG 30150

Larry Boylan is seen holding the catch of the day, which stood taller than his young son Jerry, who is pulling away from the fresh catch. *Courtesy Jerry Boylan.*

Opposite, top: This Coast Guard boat, photographed in the mid-1950s, was used to transport personnel to and from the mainland for supplies and liberty. *Courtesy Jerry Boylan.*

Opposite, bottom: Larry Boylan, an avid fisherman and diver, is seen in his wetsuit. By his side are his young children, Vicky and Jerry. *Courtesy Jerry Boylan.*

The Fresnel lens illuminated the waters for fifty-seven years until it was removed from service in 1989. A modern, solar-powered acrylic lens was put in its place. The Fresnel lens is currently on display and beautifully preserved by the Park Service in the Anacapa Visitor Center.

Adventures were many on the island. One day, the Coast Guard crew looked out the window and noticed an airplane in their backyard. They went out to investigate and found a pilot who had made an unexpected landing and was told to quickly depart or face possible consequences—of course, not before a photo was snapped.

Left: In 1989, after fifty-seven years in service, the Fresnel lens was taken out of service and is currently on display for visitors to see up close in the Visitor's Center. *Author's collection.*

Below, from left: the unnamed pilot, John Freie, Robert Remington, Don Simpson, Larry Boylan with Vicky and Jerry, Lois Boylan, Muriel Remington and Shirley Whaley. *Courtesy Jerry Boylan.*

Opposite, top: Coast Guardsman Leo Whaley posing with the Boylan family on the lower dock of Anacapa Cove. *Courtesy Jerry Boylan.*

Coast Guard buoy tender bringing fresh water to the island. *Courtesy Jerry Boylan.*

Coast Guard approaching Anacapa Island. *Courtesy Jerry Boylan.*

In 1967, the light was fully automated, and in 1970, the Coast Guard and National Park Service signed a cooperative agreement. In addition, a rescue facility was also established at Point Hueneme Light Station. The National Park Service rangers currently occupy the residential quarters and operate the other buildings; the Coast Guard operates the lighthouse and fog signal building.

In 1989, the light and foghorn were converted to solar power. In 1992, $325,000 was allocated by the Coast Guard for a complete lighthouse renovation, and in 1993, the USCGC *Conifer* embarked on a large solarization project. Periodic maintenance has been required throughout, along with a week spent rewiring the lighthouse in February 2002, led by Coast Guard chief petty officer John Stercks.

National Park Service

Today, the largest breeding colony of the endangered California brown pelican is reserved on West Anacapa. Sea birds are abundant on the island, including western gulls and several species of cormorants, a medium to large bird with usually dark feathers and a long, thin, hooked bill.

Merrill McCauley (left) and Clay Pelton, park rangers with the Channel Islands National Park. *Courtesy Kim Castro-Bran.*

Merrill McCauley serves as a law enforcement park ranger with the Channel Islands National Park. Along with other rangers, his job is to protect the wildlife and natural resources of the park, as well as ensure the safety of its visitors. He patrols by boat all five islands within the park.

About spending large amounts of time on the island, McCauley reflected, "When living on the Channel Islands, you really get to appreciate the solitude and peacefulness of living in a national park, especially one that is an island park. The loud noises you become accustomed to living in the city disappear and are replaced by the sounds of waves crashing and the call of the seabirds as they fly overhead."

He added, "Admittedly, after a while you do miss your friends and family and feel a bit disconnected from the mainland with no reliable source of communication, but it's definitely worth it to be able to live in such a beautiful place. Not many people I know get to wake up to whales jumping in their front yard!"

Visiting the Island

The lure of the lighthouse and the island and his love of the sea would continually pull Jerry Boylan, who spent some of his youth on the islands while his father was stationed there. Jerry started with his own sailboat, went on to manage Santa Barbara Boat Rentals and obtained his SCUBA certification. It was, however, following boating classes through the Coast Guard Auxiliary that Jerry pursued and acquired his captain's license in 1985. Jerry joined Truth Aquatics in 1983. Based in Santa Barbara, California, Truth Aquatics is an award-winning, multi-day live-aboard island excursion company with a simple philosophy as mentioned on their website, "Provide the best Santa Barbara Channel Islands diving, kayaking, and island hiking experience available." Just one day spent on the vessel *Conception* solidifies this philosophy. Jerry currently commands the *Conception* and also pilots all of

Jerry Boylan, son of Larry Boylan, is seen on a motor boat pulling away from the islands. *Courtesy Jerry Boylan.*

Jerry Boylan, seen here sitting on a rock taking in the splendor of the islands. *Courtesy Jerry Boylan.*

the Truth Aquatics live-aboard vessels when needed. For a full schedule of departures (off the coast of both Southern and Central California), please visit www.truthaquatics.com. Hiking is also provided in and around the Channel Islands National Park and Marine Sanctuary.

Jerry provides a unique adventure through the expertise of someone who has lived on and frequented the Channel Islands, hiked across the vast and rugged terrain, dived the diverse coasts and explored the vast caves. For Jerry, there is something about getting away from city life that allows his soul to breathe. After a few days on the mainland, Jerry is ready to head back to the islands.

Traditional amenities that usually follow an island voyage are absent, as the natural splendor of the island is undisturbed by commercial development. One advantage of this is being able to witness the island in its raw beauty; the drawback, however, is the absence of creature comforts. During the crossing to the islands, a continental breakfast is served, followed by an elaborate lunch spread later in the day. The cruise stays on schedule, with allowances for any brief stops sighting whales, dolphins or any interesting marine life that may surface.

"Every day is a challenge. It's always different," Jerry explains. "Everything is so fast in everyday life, and people are constantly rushing. Everybody's in a hurry. Out here, I see how people first come aboard anxious, but then they start to adjust, to relax. It's a transformation from when they first got here, but it takes a little time. It also takes a willingness to let go."

For those who are seeking a "Pirates of the Caribbean" at Disneyland experience, where the thrill of the boat ride lasts for about fifteen minutes and the boat is self-propelled, these adventures are quite the opposite. On these excursions, you need to be aware, alert and responsible for you first. Experienced guides are always close and are quick to radio back to the boat.

A separate company operates the kayak excursions. Even for the experienced kayakers, everyone can benefit from a refresher, as navigating in and out of the caves, especially when the swells start to pick up, can be tricky. In addition, the caves are very dark, but effective portable lights used by the guides help to brightly illuminate the cave walls.

Santa Cruz Island's Painted Cave offers visitors an awe-inspiring experience into one of the world's largest and deepest sea caves. Painted is an appropriate name for the cave as it is vibrant in color, a natural occurrence caused by algae and fungus. It is so close to the mainland, yet it is removed in that there is a feeling of raw discovery. Painted Cave is located on the northwest coastline of the island. The cave is nearly a quarter mile long and one hundred feet wide. A waterfall cascades over the entrance of the cave in the spring.

Anacapa is the ideal locale for a half- or full-day trip or a short overnight camping trip for those who like to take in the night sky without area lights obstructing the view. It must be noted that all supplies need to be brought to the island prior to arrival. As mentioned in the charter vessels' brochures, "There are no remedies for poor planning once you have arrived."

Landing Cove at East Island is available for landings. There is a staircase leading out of the cove up a steep cliffside that arrives at a figure eight–shaped trail system that is about two miles long. Middle and West Anacapa are not open to hiking, as they are preserved for wildlife

Chapter 6

LONG BEACH LIGHTHOUSE (ROBOT LIGHT)

The Port of Long Beach is wholly located in the city of Long Beach. The Port of Los Angeles, on the other hand, is composed of three distinct areas—San Pedro, Wilmington and Harbor City—which were annexed by the city of Los Angeles and went on to form the port area known today as Port of LA. These harbors are neighbors, but at the same time, they are also competitors, competing for the business of the varied cargoes that make their way in and out of the ports, most notably the large amount of containerized cargo transported by over a dozen maritime carriers. The Port of Long Beach is shielded on the west side by bluffs extending to Point Fermin. On the south side, including the southwest and southeast, the harbor is unencumbered.

A caption from the local *Long Beach Gazette* read, "This harbor means prosperity to you," a very clear way of showing its residents that they would directly benefit from this progress of the construction of the Port of Long Beach. The caption continued, "The era of the Pacific is at hand. If Long Beach is to get her share of the vast Oriental and South American trade which is knocking at her door, she must prepare for it NOW. The superstructure of our harbor has been built…and built well. It remains now but to provide the finishing touches to give Long Beach one of the finest ports on the Pacific Coast." Long Beach began construction of a government breakwater at San Pedro in 1899. Four years later, the federal government appropriated $300,500 for the construction of the inner harbor of Wilmington, deep in the San Pedro Bay.

Artist depiction of the new harbor. *Courtesy Long Beach Library History Collection.*

Public interest and investments were also increasing, and in 1905, the Los Angeles Dock and Terminal Company was formed. By the following year, development of a private harbor was already underway, known today as the Long Beach inner harbor.

Progress was moving at a fast pace, and in 1908, the War Department gave approval for a connecting channel, which is known today as the Cerritos Channel. This would connect Long Beach and Los Angeles inner harbors through the Cerritos Slough. This would further help facilitate movement of vessels in the area.

In 1909, a municipal bond issue was passed in the amount of $245,000 for the completion of a harbor. The bond money was crucial in order for the city to purchase land and was also allocated for the construction of a municipal wharf, known today as Pier 1. In addition, there was enough in bond funds for the completion of a transit shed and other facilities. It would be just a short two years until the first cargo ship docked at the municipal wharf and unloaded its shipment of lumber. The Port of Long Beach was created in June 1911.

"In 1913–1914, so destructive were the floods that many forecast the end of port growth." The district of the Los Angeles County Flood Control was established to find solutions to this devastating situation. The federal government also rendered aid, and a silt diversion channel was completed in 1923.

Cargo being unloaded at the Port of Long Beach. *Courtesy Long Beach Library History Collection.*

With the floods seemingly under control, attention turned back to port development, and in 1924, voters approved a $5 million bond issue for harbor development. This was a huge victory for the city. Wasting no time, a breakwater was constructed, extending near the flood control channel into the ocean. Two moles (man-made peninsulas within a harbor or port) were also constructed. Known today as the Navy Mole, they were necessary in order to protect the harbor entrance.

Seeing the rapid progress, voters also approved another $2.7 million, only four years after the initial bond of $5 million. The municipal wharf already needed improvements, so monies from the new bond were used for repairs and reconstruction. In addition, they were able to construct further piers, wharves and other facilities.

Following construction, it was reported that 2 million tons of cargo moved through the port. The tonnage of cargo was soon to expand in 1930, when a new transit shed was constructed, along with an additional shed in 1935. They were utilized to accompany a rail line, which was connected to the Pacific Electric, Southern and Union Pacific railways. That same year work began for Pier A; Berths 1, 2 and 3; Pier B; and Berths 11, 12, 12A and 1B.

The Port of Long Beach would see fifteen- to twenty-foot waves crashing over its breakwater on April 22, 1930. The *Long Beach Press Telegram* reported, "The disturbance was connected with the tidal wave off the coast of Mexico." Fortunately, loss was at a minimum.

On July 3, 1930, the United States Congress passed and President Herbert Hoover signed into law the Rivers and Harbors Bill. This would be critical to future harbor development. President Hoover stated, "It was with particular satisfaction that I signed the Rivers and Harbors Bill, as it represents the final authorization of the engineering work by which we construct and coordinate our great systems of waterways and harbors, which I have advocated for over five years. It was promised in the last campaign and in my recommendations to Congress." In doing so, necessary funds and support were authorized for harbor improvements. The federal breakwater was extended across San Pedro Bay during World War II.

At first glance, Long Beach Lighthouse resembles more of a Lego construction than that of a lighthouse, and with various buoy markers, barges and passing ships in the area, the structure gets lost in the background, causing it to be often overlooked. The usual reaction when the lighthouse is

Long Beach Lighthouse following construction in 1949. It consists of a reinforced concrete blockhouse and tower fifty-five feet high. *Courtesy Eric Castro-Bran.*

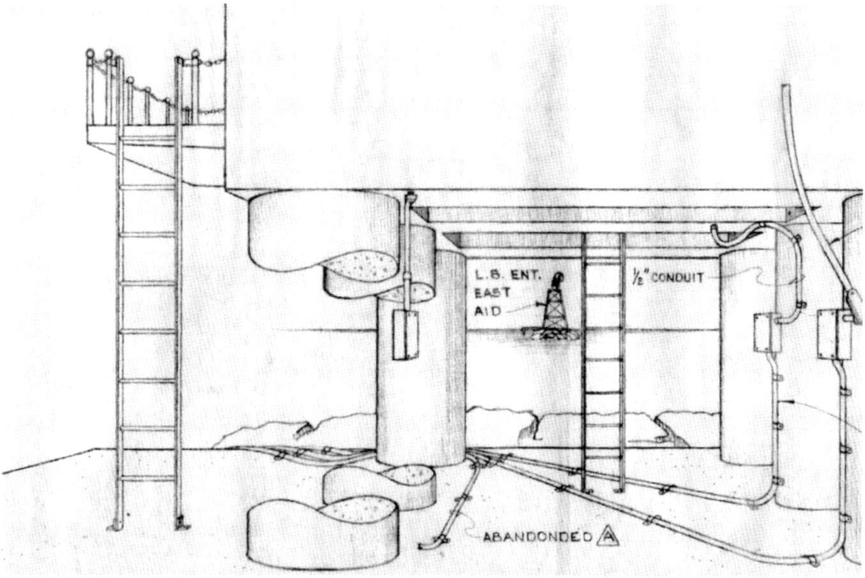

The blueprint illustrates the bottom half of the Long Beach Lighthouse. *Courtesy Eric Castro-Bran.*

pointed out is first a double take, followed by, "That's a lighthouse?" The boxy, stout, forty-two-foot-high, monolithic structure, sad to say, does leave a lot to be desired, and with whispers of a redesign for years, change is most likely on the horizon.

Unlike its neighboring lighthouses, photo ops have been far and few between. But popularity aside, this lighthouse structure has proven to be a trustworthy seafaring guidepost for well over fifty years. Every detail had to be taken into consideration, with over a year of planning and testing before construction could even begin.

The design included six large steel pilings, which were constructed onto a platform anchoring it to the breakwater foundation in order to help secure the structure and shield it from impending waves and storms. The leggy appearance of the columns helped coin its affectionate nickname "Robot Light." A submarine cable feed (2,400 volts) extended from Pier J in Long Beach and stretched along the harbor floor to the lighthouse. This cable was installed in 1966 and was used in place of generators. Since then, the cable has been damaged routinely.

Completed in 1949, the lighthouse sits on the federal breakwater adjacent to the "Queen's Gate" entrance to Long Beach harbor. It was designed to withstand earthquakes and seismic tidal waves and has proved its structural

A ceremony taking place at the Coast Guard Offices when the offices were first located in Long Beach. *Courtesy U.S. Coast Guard.*

soundness as it has survived decades of ocean bombardment without having ever suffered any major damage from a storm. It was built of reinforced concrete with walls six inches thick at a cost of about $100,000.

The design was entrusted to the U.S. Coast Guard Engineering Department, Eleventh Coast Guard District in Long Beach, California. The designing engineers were Commander E.W. Laird and C.N. Coseboom (who served as the senior civil engineers), and John T. Hendrix was the chief electrician. The plans included the lighthouse structure; the foghorn, along with a spare foghorn; and a radio beacon. The optic ranged up to twenty miles out to sea and consisted of a rotating carriage into which four bulbs are fitted. The carriage brings a new bulb into position automatically if the one in use burns out.

This well-crafted beacon, in its time, was touted as the pinnacle of lighthouse technology and was said to be the world's first fully automatic lighthouse. It was simple yet functional. Lighthouse keepers especially took notice as the lighthouse was designed to be self-contained during a time when all other Coast Guard lighthouses were still being manned and regularly maintained. This was a technological advancement in a major aid to navigation. A unique aspect of having a fully automated lighthouse is that a galley, living area and berthing areas were no longer necessary. This also played a huge role in the new design, which now focused solely on the utilitarian aspects of the light, foghorn and radio beacon. Some of the equipment in the lighthouse would operate automatically, while other devices were radio controlled from the Los Angeles lighthouse, only five miles away.

The building itself showcased this new freedom, as architects and engineers were able to design the structure itself to serve as part of the radio beacon's ground plane (part of the beacon's transmitter antenna array). Sitting atop the lighthouse was a steel tower, which became known as the "Eiffel Tower" antenna. It once served as the antenna of the radio beacon. In the early 1970s, the light was modernized and new monitoring equipment was installed. The radio beacon was discontinued in 1992.

As you look from the outside of the lighthouse with its rectangle bottom and linear-square top, it appears to be only a two-story structure, but once inside the lighthouse, it is quite evident that it is actually three stories and much roomier than imagined.

The usual comforts of a lighthouse with a staircase were also abandoned, opting for a vertical wall-attached, steel ladder with only a heavy push-up metal lid, designed to keep moisture out. Originally, the first floor was fitted

The USS *Eversole* (DD-789) is seen here passing the Long Beach Lighthouse on its way out to sea. The *Eversole* was a Gearing-class destroyer of the U.S. Navy. It was named in honor of Lieutenant Junior Grade John Eversole, a naval aviator killed in World War II. *Courtesy U.S. Coast Guard.*

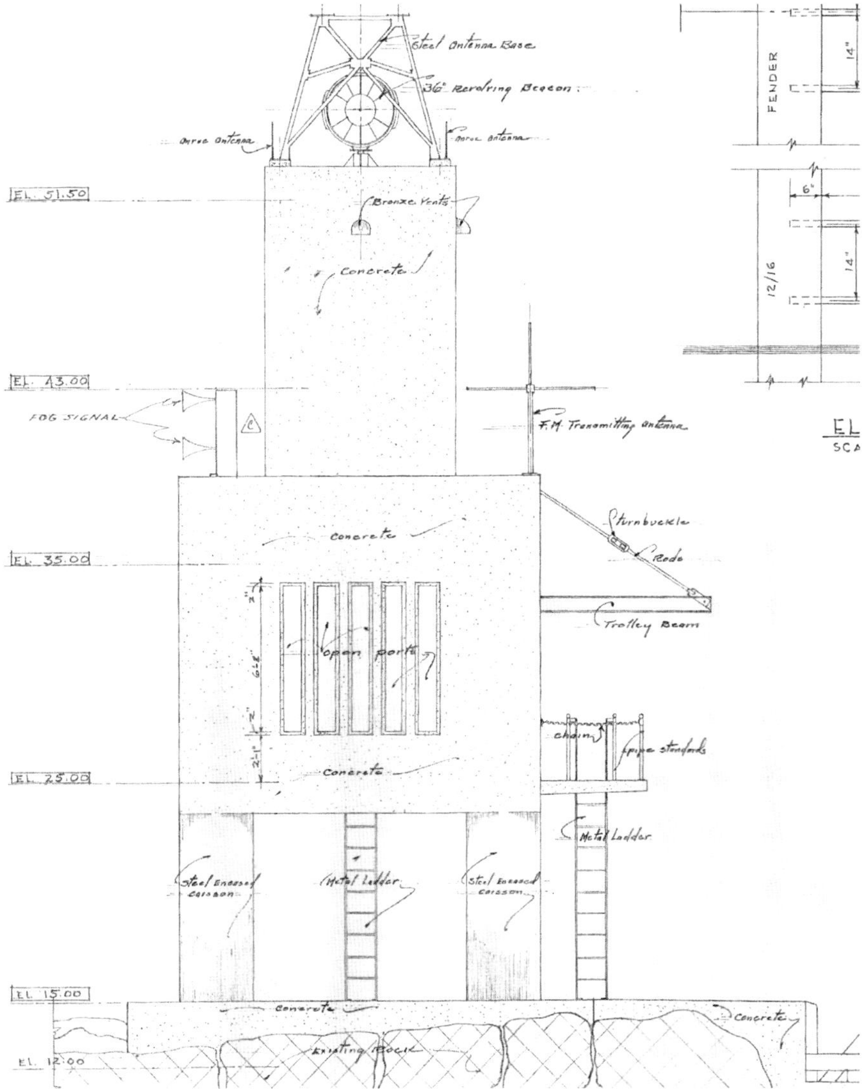

The blueprint illustrates the lighthouse structure and its supporting foundation. *Courtesy Eric Castro-Bran.*

with diesel generators sets and equipped with master control panels, which were programmed with cycle timers that would automatically start the generators every four hours, as well as external fuel tanks.

The double-compressed, air-driven, seventeen-inch Tyfon foghorns were controlled by radio from Los Angeles Lighthouse only five miles away using the new Aids to Navigation Radio Control system (ANRAC). The system was developed during the war so that coastal aids could be turned off if in fear of impending attack and turned on for friendly ships. It was housed on the second floor, with the double-horned fog signal on the roof of the first box structure. The foghorn proved its effectiveness in 1955, when it made a world record after the steamship *Talamanca* recoded hearing the foghorn thirty-three miles out at sea. The third floor was used for the radio beacon transmitter.

It was equipped with a thirty-six-inch airway or aero-type beacon, which, like the fog signal, was controlled by the ANRAC system from Los Angeles Lighthouse. This was not the traditional lamp used by area lighthouses, but a one-thousand-watt, 140,000 candle power all-weather rotating airway beacon mounted on the roof. An astronomical clock located at the top would turn the light on and off using a trigger mechanism. Looking to the stars, this switching mechanism would automatically adjust based on daylight hours.

In addition to the ANRAC system, the light was also outfitted with a ratchet system. Once the system detects that the light is burned out, it ratchets or

BM2 Joseph Hinds and MK1 Jeremy Hinis of the Coast Guards Aids to Navigation Team Los Angeles/Long Beach (ANT LA/LB) heading out of the Coast Guard base in Terminal Island in their "TAM-B" boat to service a navigational aid. *Courtesy Kim Castro-Bran.*

A replacement lens is being lifted by electrician's mate and executive officer Christopher Robinson of the Aids to Navigation Team (ANT LA/LB) to the top of the light. *Courtesy Kim Castro-Bran.*

A recent view of the lighthouse, illustrating the signs of wear and tear of the elements of nature. *Courtesy Kim Castro-Bran.*

switches position and a new light takes its place. The light contained a thirty-six-inch lens and could be seen at a distance of thirteen miles.

Even though it has never been manned, one benefit of the proximity of this lighthouse is that it is only a short boat ride away from the Terminal Island Coast Guard station. The Coast Guard Aids to Navigation team continues to operate the station and perform regular maintenance.

The lighthouse, which had transitioned from generators to submarine cables, would see its greatest advancement, solarization, which has proven to be the most cost-effective and environmentally friendly alternative for safe and effective navigation. This extensive undertaking was performed by the crew of the Coast Guard cutter *Conifer* in 1993, at a cost of $45,000, and was completed in a two-week time frame. The *Conifer* is a 180-foot buoy tender based in San Pedro and services the Federal Aids to Navigation between San Simeon and the Mexican border.

All the outdated equipment had to first be stripped from the lighthouse along with interior renovations. A total of sixteen solar panels were mounted on the south face of the structure, and a power distribution system was installed in order to charge the large storage batteries and monitor the power supply to the lens and fog signal. In addition to the ratchet system that rotates the lamp or light bulb, the auxiliary light works on the same premise and turns on automatically if the main light should go out.

Talks of replacing the lighthouse have circulated for years, and in the future, this once state-of-the-art aid to navigation will undoubtedly be replaced. The lighthouse can be viewed from many of the local harbor excursions.

Chapter 7

LIONS LIGHTHOUSE FOR SIGHT

Since ancient times, lighthouses have been an integral part of the development of the maritime trade around the world, yet equally encompassing is their legacy of lifesaving heroism. One organization built on helping others is the Lions Club International, whose founder, Melvin Jones, lived by the motto, "You can't get very far until you start doing something for somebody else." Born on January 13, 1879, Melvin dedicated much of his eighty-two years of life striving to help others. Founded on June 7, 1917, the Lions Club has expanded to over two hundred countries, sharing this simple yet selfless philosophy.

To clarify, the Lions Lighthouse for Sight has been commonly referred to in books and reports as the Long Beach Lighthouse, but it is not. The Long Beach Lighthouse, as discussed in the previous chapter, is a federal aid to navigation. The Lions Lighthouse for Sight serves as a private aid to navigation. The lighthouse is, however, noted on the maritime publication *Light List*, is a significant landmark and is also quite a popular tourist attraction in the city of Long Beach.

When the city of Long Beach was looking to erect a lighthouse, members of the downtown Long Beach Lions Club seized the opportunity to have a beacon shine out to the community that they desire to serve. This dream, however, came with a steep price. The club was given the green light, provided that it could raise a large amount of money in a short time frame. Immediately, the challenge seemed daunting and almost out of reach. But the representation of this great lighthouse monument, which would shine light into the darkness, also represented one of the group's fundamental missions: bringing sight to those who would otherwise live in darkness.

The lighthouse was the brainchild of Bob Paternoster, director of planning for the Long Beach Aquarium and Queensway Bay Harbor Projects. Upon hearing of his lighthouse plans, Vito Romans, past Lions district governor, along with Paul Mandeville, past president of the Downtown Long Beach Lions Club, met with Bob to discuss the project.

The Lions Club had been looking for a noteworthy community service project in the city of Long Beach to help commemorate its nearly one hundred years of service. It was, however, an enormous undertaking with a price tag of over $500,000, which needed to be raised in a six-month time frame. The Lion's Club agreed to raise $200,000 and planned to request matching funds from the California Tideland's Foundation, which generates revenue from oil profits from drilling in the tidelands area of California. Monies allocated from this fund for development must be used solely within this area. The Lion's Club met and exceeded its goal within the first four months, thanks in part to local community members and businesses who, in addition to donations, also offered free printing and mailing services for the fundraising campaign. For the group's enormous efforts, the city named the new lighthouse the Lions Lighthouse for Sight.

Even with funding in place, challenges remained. The location for the new lighthouse, known as Queensway Bay, consisted of soft, loose or "uncompacted" dredge fill, which was a byproduct created in the late 1940s, when the Port of Long Beach was dredging its harbor and redistributed the excess landfill.

The surprising answer came in the form of a German paper written in the 1930s. Faced with a similar dilemma, the solution had been to create a foundation large enough that is would in fact move the center of gravity of the entire structure so that it occurs within the foundation. Consequently, a large circular concrete foundation, spanning twenty-eight feet in diameter and approximately six feet thick was constructed. Additionally, a secondary problem was solved, because in the event of an earthquake, any settlement will be in the vertical direction only, with zero rotation of the structure.

The construction would not be complete without first holding an official ceremony. The public was invited for the full regalia, and the welcoming brochure stated, "The Lions Lighthouse for Sight will tower 100 feet into the Long Beach Skyline, guarding the entrance to the City's newest coastal attraction, Rainbow Harbor. The lighthouse is scheduled to be completed in July of 2000, when it becomes fully operational and home to a full-time

Lions Lighthouse for Sight, with its conical and tapered tower. *Courtesy Kim Castro-Bran.*

Harbor Master. Please join us in celebrating the groundbreaking of the newest and brightest landmark on our city's magnificent coastline."

The ceremony kicked off with the Long Beach Junior Concert Band, followed by opening remarks from the city manager, Henry Taboada. Mayor Beverly O'Neill gave welcoming remarks and introduced Vito Romans, who recognized the long list of contributors. It was through these contributors that within a short time, the lighthouse was made possible. Four of the top benefactors generously donated $20,000 or more, followed by close to 250 benefactors of various contributions.

One characteristic of the Lions Lighthouse for Sight is that there is a significant widening at the base of the lighthouse, and as it extends toward the sky, there is obvious tapering or narrowing of this conical structure. This is true for all cylindrically styled lighthouses, though usually not as apparent.

The shape is a consequence of Mother Nature or, more specifically, the wind. As wind blows around a vertical cylindrical structure, it creates vortices or a mass of whirling air, also called eddies. This phenomenon is known as the Von Kármán Effect or the Kármán Vortex, named after Theodore von Kármán, a Hungarian physicist who discovered this natural phenomenon.

This bombardment of swirling air mass has caused buildings to vibrate sideways perpendicular to the direction of the wind, resulting in destruction and devastation. The solution to counterbalance this effect is to simply change the shape of the structure—in this case, from a straight vertical cylinder to that of a tapered structure, larger at the base, smaller at the top. At the base, the lighthouse is fourteen feet in diameter; at the circular platform, eight feet in diameter; height to the base of the platform, fifty-four feet, eight inches; height of the lens enclosure, ten feet, eight inches; total height, sixty-five feet, four inches.

Dennis Drag, PhD, who is a member of the downtown Long Beach Lions Club, was the project manager and engineer responsible for the design of the Lions Lighthouse for Sight. He was an associate vice-president at Moffatt and Nichol, a multi-disciplined engineering firm with its corporate office located in Long Beach, California. Dennis was responsible for the firm's infrastructure projects, managing and directing numerous one-of-a-kind mega projects, including the John Wayne Airport project.

When the firm completed the Queensway Bay harbor project, the city asked Moffatt and Nichol to design the proposed iconic lighthouse. With the harbor project completed on site, construction needed to be minimized. Code implications limited the lighthouse to its current maximum height. Dennis, having extensive prior experience in vessel design, recommended to the city that a prefabricated, internally stiffened conical shell

Dennis Drag, PhD, seen in front of the Long Beach Lions banner at their monthly meeting. *Author's collection.*

structure was the most cost-effective for the lighthouse. The city agreed with the firm's recommendations, and the rest is history.

A steel conical structure was used, which helped in compliance for both the static and dynamic earthquake analysis required in the design process. The entire lighthouse structure was shop fabricated, painted and shipped to the site, ready for a very dramatic and quick erection by Paramount Metal and Supply Company. It was delivered in three sections: the conical steel shell, the cylindrical platform and the lens enclosure. All three sections were delivered to the site at night, and at a glance, it looked similar to that of a rocket assembly. The following daylight was used to early erect the tower, with three separate crane lifts used to install the entire lighthouse structure. Amazingly, the entire assembly was completed in twenty minutes.

Inside the lighthouse is a cage access ladder, which is both permanently and vertically mounted inside with platforms at various elevations allowing for maintenance and cleaning of the lens enclosure. The electrical equipment for the lighthouse and lighting system are located on a platform just above what is called the harbor master's office. The office was a requirement of the state's Department of Boats and Waterways (DBW). DBW provided the city a financial grant toward the cost of the lighthouse project. However, the office would never be occupied by the harbor master for myriad reasons.

Similar in color to the other area lighthouses, the Lions Lighthouse for Sight is also white with a red lantern room and black railings. A white entrance door is surrounded by black-framed windows and a gray base. There is a paved spiral walkway leading to the lighthouse. The owner/site manager of the lighthouse is the City of Long Beach.

Where it differs in color is at the base of the lighthouse, where there are eight programmable light fixtures, which are tied into the Queensway Bay Harbor audio system. At night, as music is played, the lights will illuminate and, as they change color, appear to dance to the beat of the music. For those who are able to visit the Queensway Bay Harbor, the ever-changing nighttime illumination to the harbor music in the evenings is breathtaking.

One pronounced difference between a federal and a private aid to navigation is the optics. Active federal lighthouses are required to maintain specific optics and light characteristics enabling the beam of light to stretch miles upon miles out to sea. The Lions Lighthouse for Sight has a simulated beacon, which consists of two lamps positioned back to back. The lamp apparatus turns 180 degrees and then rotates back to its original position, creating the effect of an actual lighthouse beacon. So as not to shine directly into adjacent office buildings, the optics were greatly reduced.

The lighthouse has an elevation of approximately 110 feet and is situated on a peninsula that encompasses the Shoreline Aquatic Park. The surrounding waters by the lighthouse include Queensway Bay to the south, Rainbow Harbor to the north and the Los Angeles River to the west. The area surrounding the lighthouse is protected from any future development, making it an ideal family-fun center. Visitors have posted comments online, such as: "Benches all around. Have a seat and enjoy the view"; "The perfect

The lantern room of the Lions Lighthouse for Sight in Long Beach. *Courtesy Kim Castro-Bran.*

place to curl up with a book"; "Take a bike and ride to the lighthouse at night and watch the light dance on the water and maybe you'll get lucky and spot some dolphins or seals in the bay"; and "Fantastic view of downtown and harbor."

The park is known for its amazing views of the *Queen Mary*, the Long Beach skyline and the Aquarium of the Pacific (located next door). The aquarium is the largest in Southern California, with a mission to "instill a sense of wonder, respect, and stewardship for the Pacific Ocean, its inhabitants, and ecosystems." There is so much to see, take in and experience in every direction. Along with the Rainbow Harbor/Rainbow Marina located next to the Aquarium of the Pacific, local attractions also include whale watching, dinner cruises, private charters, sport fishing, boat rentals and much more. Shoreline Village overlooks Rainbow Marina with arcades, shops and restaurants, to name a few.

The *Queen Mary* and the Lions Lighthouse for Sight are separated by the Los Angeles River. On October 31, 1967, the *Queen Mary* set out for its final voyage and, just over a month later, on December 9, 1967, called Long Beach, California, its new and permanent home. The *Queen Mary* is now a floating spacious hotel equipped with fun events and attraction. It is also renowned for its three world-class restaurants and is a Southern California icon.

The Parkers' Lighthouse restaurant is commonly thought to be an actual lighthouse and has been confused with Lions Lighthouse for Sight, which is nearby. Parkers' Lighthouse is solely a restaurant. The restaurant was established in 1983 and is best known for its daily fresh seafood selection and specialty items.

Outreach and Visiting

Lion's member Gene Johnson reflected on the club's recent outreach to help a single mother of three, suffering from near blindness due to cataracts, gain her sight back. With the help of volunteer doctors and contributors, a procedure that would have cost over $60,000 was made available at a cost of only $6,000 to the organization. All the prep work, phone calls and requests for help were worth it all when they witnessed the young mother look into her children's faces and wrap her arms around them. Overcoming insurmountable obstacles and giving sight to those who would otherwise never see is what the group is all about, and dreaming big permeates through all its endeavors.

The Lions Club continues to look to the future and embrace opportunities to help not only the community but also the environment and the future of the planet. The group is continually looking to younger generations to continue its service and legacy.

Lions Lighthouse for Sight is located at 200 Aquarium Way (in Shoreline Aquatic Park) in Long Beach. Shoreline Aquatic Park is a city park on Queensway Bay near downtown Long Beach. The lighthouse is located just to the east of the Aquarium of the Pacific, on the north side of the entrance to Long Beach Harbor and the west side of the small boat basin.

Chapter 8

U.S. COAST GUARD

Keepers of the Light

On August 4, 1790, Congress passed and George Washington signed a bill that allotted for ten boats whose duty would be to guard the coast against smugglers. Referred to as the Revenue Marine, followed by the Revenue Cutter Service, it was in 1915 that the guardians of the coast would officially be called the United States Coast Guard. From its original inception in 1790, the Coast Guard continues to fulfill its duties, making it the oldest of the nation's seagoing armed forces.

A fleet of armed cutters would be next in line, thanks to Alexander Hamilton, the first secretary of the treasury and also known as the father of the Coast Guard. This ensured that vessels entering the waters of the United States would pay tonnage dues and import dues.

Hamilton had an uphill battle, as smuggling was considered a patriotic act against the British "taxation without representation" and had led to the Boston Tea Party of December 16, 1773. Following the revolution, smuggling was commonplace and went undeterred. But for the young nation to survive, Hamilton was forced to press on and convince the people that taxation *with* representation was in their best interest. Hamilton did not back down but instead enforced custom laws by growing the Coast Guard to a fleet. Soon, smuggling would be less profitable and appealing. Between 1795 and 1801, the original ten boats were gradually phased out, and thirteen larger ships, complete with facilities, an established crew and more gun power, were in place.

In 1798, President John Adams was aware that Congress was going to extend the scope of the Coast Guard. Realizing that this change was eminent, President Adams was quick to appoint Benjamin Stoddert as the first secretary of the navy. This came at a good time, as tensions with France were increasing on the waters and an undeclared shooting battle at sea broke out. As French privateers captured more than 340 American ships, Congress, as President John Adams anticipated, declared in 1799, "Revenue Cutters shall, whenever the President of the United States shall so direct, cooperate with the Navy of the United States."

The legacy of the U.S. Coast Guard in the West began with the U.S. Lighthouse Service. Congress, understanding that safe navigation was paramount for development of the West, gave authorization in 1848 for the establishment of lighthouses along the barren coast.

On August 4, 1949, Congress further declared, "That Coast Guard as established January 28, 1915, shall be a military service and a branch of the armed forces of the United States at all times. The Coast Guard shall be a service in the Treasury Department, except when operating as a service in the Navy."

For over two centuries, this highly visible armada and the core missions of Coast Guard have coincided with our nation's demand. This was especially evident in response to the terrorist attacks of September 11, 2001. The Coast Guard went into overdrive, protecting our shores with a visibility compared to that of World War II. The role of homeland-security operations post 9/11 created an immediate change in mission priorities.

The Coast Guard is a military, multi-mission, maritime service within the Department of Homeland Security. Its core roles are to protect the public, the environment and the U.S. economic and security interests in any maritime region in which those interests may be at risk, including international waters and America's coasts, ports and inland waters.

The Coast Guard exercises a mix of military, humanitarian and civilian law-enforcement roles. The Coast Guard has five fundamental roles: maritime safety, maritime security, maritime mobility, national defense and protection of natural resources. It maintains a presence on navigable waterways of all the coastlines of the United States. The Coast Guard is one of five armed services and is tasked with several missions. The eleven statutory missions as defined by law are divided into homeland security missions and non-homeland security missions.

Non-homeland security missions are composed of marine safety, search and rescue, aids to navigation, living marine resources (fisheries law enforcement), marine environmental protection and ice operations.

Homeland security missions include ports, waterways and coastal security; drug interdiction; migrant interdiction; defense readiness; and other law enforcement.

Navigable channels must continually be kept up and marked appropriately, keeping the flow of incoming and outgoing traffic moving safely.

The goal of the Coast Guard is to have all aids to navigation at a 98 percent workability rate, giving mariners constant guidance and warnings.

The *George Cobb* is the fourteenth and final "keeper class" coastal buoy tender built by Marinette Marine Corporation in Marinette, Wisconsin. The "keeper class" cutters are named in honor of famous lighthouse keepers of the past and are commissioned to primarily service buoys in Los Angeles, Long Beach, San Diego and San Francisco Harbors.

The *George Cobb* was launched on December 18, 1999, and was placed, per the Coast Guard, "In Commission, Special" status on June 22, 2000. It would then make a 108-day voyage of nine thousand nautical miles through the Great Lakes, St. Lawrence Seaway, down the East Coast and around Central America via the Panama Canal. The *George Cobb* had its formal commissioning ceremony in San Pedro, California, on October 27, 2000. As the Coast Guard works with a total force of just over forty-five thousand men and women, the *George Cobb* has also expanded far beyond the previous scope of previous buoy tenders. Its missions include search and rescue, homeland defense, maritime law enforcement, marine environmental protection and ice breaking.

This particular cutter is named for George D. Cobb, who served as the second assistant keeper for Point Bonita Lighthouse, which is located at the entrance to San Francisco Bay. While alone in the tower on the stormy night of December 26, 1896, George Cobb spotted a capsized sailboat at the entrance to the bay. Realizing that there was no time for the closest lifesaving station to render assistance, George manned a station boat alone and rowed though the surf to the offshore reefs. He single-handedly pulled two men into the boat, pulled one man off the rocks and then landed all three safely back at the lighthouse. George Cobb is remembered not only for this heroic act but also for being one of only a few members of the Lighthouse Service to earn the Silver Life Saving Medal.

Saving lives is the ultimate goal of the Coast Guard. One of the best ways it achieves this is setting and enforcing boating safety standards. The Coast Guard also utilizes that Coast Guard Auxiliary, a volunteer arm of the Coast Guard, to get out the message of boating safety. Offering an array of classes for the boating public and free vessel-safety checks and also sponsoring boating events and public outreach, the Coast Guard can achieve an even broader reach of education and prevention.

Serving the maritime trade and general boating public in the Los Angeles/Long Beach area is Base Support Command (BSC) San Pedro, which is located on an extension of Terminal Island in San Pedro, California. Terminal Island was originally called La Isla de La Culebra de Cascabel, or Rattlesnake Island, a name befitting the many cold-blooded creatures basking in the California sun while at the same time warning anyone who sets foot on its shore. The inception of Coast Guard Base Terminal Island came about in the early 1950s, following the construction of the boat basin, barracks and administration building

The southwest corner of Terminal Island, known as Reservation Point, was developed from dredging excess soil during channel expansion. Prior to World War II, Reservation Point was used as an immigration and naturalization service processing center and a U.S. Public Health Service quarantine station. In addition, it housed the Lighthouse Service industrial depot, once home to the U.S. Lighthouse Service. The former lighthouse depot building is still standing and today serves as a machine shop on base and also the Coast Guard Buoy Depot.

Coast Guard ANT boat approaches Long Beach Lighthouse. *Courtesy Kim Castro-Bran.*

During the war, the navy established a brig. The term "brig" was a carry-over from navy vessels as the brig is located at the bow of the ship and was used as a holding cell or jail for the navy. The brig would expand into a medium security federal prison, which is still situated on the eastern half of Reservation Point.

In walking distance from the former lighthouse depot building is offices of the Coast Guard Aids to Navigation Team Los Angeles/Long Beach. There are specialized teams within the Coast Guard challenged to meet the needs of a wide arrange of beacons. They are commonly referred to as the ANT or ANT Team, short for Aids to Navigation Team, and were established on April 18, 1986. (There are multiple ANT units throughout the United States and territories, but in LA/LB, there is only one unit.) Their mascot is an ant and is typically seen holding a light bulb standing next to Point Vicente Lighthouse in Rancho Palos Verdes, California—an appropriate mascot as the team routinely arrives at the light needing repair, carries in or removes large pieces of equipment, repairs the light and usually leaves without anyone realizing that the light had gone out in the first place.

The mission of the Aids to Navigation Team Los Angeles/Long Beach is the establishment, maintenance and servicing of aids to navigations

Coast Guard ANT unit getting underway from the Coast Guard Base Terminal Island. *Courtesy Kim Castro-Bran.*

(ATONs, or Aids TO Navigation) in the Los Angeles/Long Beach area of responsibility (AOR). This area covers over three hundred miles of California coastline from Morrow Bay in the north to Dana Point in the south and encompasses eight offshore islands. Lighthouses included in this area are San Luis Obispo, Point Arguello, Point Conception, Santa Barbara, Anacapa, Point Hueneme, Point Vicente Point Fermin, Los Angeles (Angel's Gate), Long Beach (Queen's Gate) and Point Loma.

Since 1939, as the Coast Guard merged with and assumed the duties of the Lighthouse Service, it has continued operations. As the Aids to Navigation Team makes its way up and down the coast to service these aids, a preventative maintenance service is routinely done in ordered to help ensure continued service. Each service is completed with a thorough checklist and recording of the day's events and items that may be of concern in the future are noted so that extra supplies and equipment can be brought up, as a precaution for the next scheduled or emergency service. They help keep mariners safe by ensuring the lights continue to wink and blink.

BIBLIOGRAPHY

Bloomfield, Howard V.L. *The Compact History of the United States Coast Guard.* New York: Hawthorn Books, 1966.

"Build Big Harbor Three Miles at Sea." *Popular Science Monthly*, December 1932.

Delgado, James P. *To California by Sea: A Maritime History of the California Gold Rush*. Columbia: University of South Carolina Press, 1990.

Fink, Augusta. *Palos Verdes Peninsula: Time and the Terraced Land.* Lafayette, CA: Great West Books, 2004.

Garnett Clark, Ginger. *Rancho Palos Verdes*. Charleston, SC: Arcadia Publishing, 2009.

Gerold, Charles, and Jack C. Miller. *Dreams That Come True.* Ventura, CA: Official Souvenir Program, 1939.

Grant, John, and Ray Jones. *Legendary Lighthouses.* Old Saybrook, CT: Globe Pequot Press, 1998.

Greenland, Powell March. *A Troubled Dream: Richard Bard's Struggle to Build a Harbor at Hueneme, California.* Los Olivos, CA: Olive Press Publications, 2006.

Hardison, J.E. "The Last Voyage of the S.S. *Dominator*." Unpublished manuscript.

Hedley, Bungy. *Time Line of San Pedro History 1542–1964*. San Pedro, CA: Trade Winds Cove Enterprises, 2010.

Holland, Ross H., Jr. *America's Lighthouses*. New York: Dover Publications, 2006.

Krythe, Maymie. *Port Admiral Phineas Banning 1830–1885*. San Francisco: California Historical Society, 1957.

Lamb, Susan. *Channel Islands National Park*. Tucson, AZ: Western National

Parks Association, 2000.

Leffingwell, Randy, and Pamela Welty. *Lighthouses of the Pacific Coast*. Stillwater, MN: Voyageur Press, 2000.

Marquez, Ernest. *Port Los Angeles: A Phenomenon of the Railroad Era*. San Marino, CA: Golden West Books, 1975.

Maulhardt, Jeffrey W. *Port Hueneme*. Charleston, SC: Arcadia Publishing, 2005.

Miller, Bruce. *The Gabrielino*. Los Osos, CA: Sand River Press, 1991.

Mosley, Henrietta E. *Point Fermin Lighthouse Families 1874–1927*. Palos Verdes, CA: Pacific Heritage Books, 2013.

Mosley, Henrietta E., and Kristen Heather. "Patronage, Politics and Preferences, Point Fermin Lighthouse Keeper Mary Smith's Truncated Career." *The Keeper's Log*, 2009.

National Park Service. *Channel Islands National Park*, Washington, D.C.: U.S. National Park Service, n.d.

Nelson, Stephen R., and David K. Appel. *Fort MacArthur*. Charleston, SC: Arcadia Publishing, 2005.

Nichols, Gina. *The Seabees at Port Hueneme*. Charleston, SC: Arcadia Publishing, 2006.

"Point Fermin Enters New Era." *Lighthouse Digest*, July 2006.

Point Fermin Lighthouse Volunteer Resource Manual. San Pedro, CA: Point Fermin Lighthouse, n.d.

Queenan, Charles F. *Long Beach and Los Angeles: A Tale of Two Ports*. Northridge, CA: Windsor Publications, Inc., 1986.

Roberts, Bruce, and Ray Jones. *Lighthouses of California*. Guilford, CT: Globe Pequot Press, 2005.

Seattle Sun Times. "Automatic Lighthouse." March 13, 1939.

Silka, Henry P. *Boomtown, San Pedro in the 1980's*. San Pedro, CA: San Pedro Bay Historical Society, 1993.

Sonneborn, Liz. *The Chumash*. Minneapolis, MN: Lerner Publications Company, 2007.

Stimson, Thomas E., Jr. "Goodbye Lighthouse Keeper." *Popular Mechanics*, September 1948.

Strobridge, Truman R. *Chronology of Aids to Navigation and the Old Lighthouse Service 1716–1939*. Washington, D.C.: U.S. Coast Guard Public Affairs Division, 1974.

Thubron, Colin, and the editors of Time-Life Books. *The Ancient Mariners*. Alexandria, VA: Time-Life Books Inc., 1981.

U.S. Coast Guard. *Lighthouses Then and Now*. Washington, D.C.: Commandant's Bulletin, USCG, 1987.

Ward, Thomas C. "Point Hueneme Lighthouse." *The Keeper's Log*, 1992.

Weymouth, Kent. "Point Vicente Light Station California." *The Keeper's Log*, 2008.

Weymouth, Kent, Powell March Greenland and Cara Converse. *The Journal of Ventura County History*. Ventura, CA: Ventura County Historical Society, Museum of Ventura County, 2010.

Wheeler, Wayne C., and the United States Lighthouse Society. *California Lighthouse Life in the 1920's and 1930's*. Charleston, SC: Arcadia Publishing, 2000.

Wheeler, Wayne C. "*Anacapa Island Light Station*." *The Keeper's Log*, 2002.

White, Michael D. *The Port of Los Angeles*. Charleston, SC: Arcadia Publishing, 2008.

Websites

Aquarium of the Pacific. www.aquariumofpacific.org.

Lighthouse Friends. www.lighthousefriends.com.

Lions Club. www.lionsclub.org.

Los Angeles Maritime Museum. www.lamaritimemuseum.org.

National Park Service. www.nps.gov.

Point Fermin Lighthouse Society. www.pfls.org.

Point Hueneme Lighthouse. www.huenemelight.org.

Point Vicente Interpretive Center. www.palosverdes.com/rpv.

Point Vicente Lighthouse. www.vicentelight.org.

The Queen Mary. www.queenmary.com.

Truth Aquatics. www.truthaquatics.com.

ABOUT THE AUTHOR

A public affairs specialist in the U.S. Coast Guard Auxiliary and a member of the U.S. Coast Guard Aids to Navigation Team Los Angeles/Long Beach, author Rose Castro-Bran helps maintain California's lighthouses and has been museum curator of Point Hueneme Lighthouse for over a decade. She is the author of the popular children's book *The Adventures of Port Herman Lighthouse* and also *Lighthouses of the Ventura Coast*. The evocative images, both vintage and current, showcased here are from her collection, local museums, area lighthouses, lighthouse keepers' families and the U.S. Coast Guard.